Ex Libris

F. Peter Cundill

Audley Twiston-Davies

....

This hardback has been privately printed, at Peter's request, by The Cundill Foundation, so that Peter's closest friends and colleagues could have a memento which we now have great pleasure in sending you.

Christopher Risso Gill

....

Christopher Risso-Gill

THERE'S ALWAYS SOMETHING TO DO

THERE'S ALWAYS SOMETHING TO DO

THE PETER CUNDILL INVESTMENT APPROACH

McGill-Queen's University Press Montreal & Kingston • London • Ithaca

ISBN 978-0-7735-3537-4 (cloth)

Legal deposit first quarter 2011
Bibliothèque nationale du Québec

Printed in Canada on acid-free paper.

McGill-Queen's University Press acknowledges the support of the Canada Council for the Arts for our publishing program. We also acknowledge the financial support of the Government of Canada through the Canada Book Fund for our publishing activities.

Library and Archives Canada Cataloguing in Publication

Risso-Gill, Christopher, 1948–
There's always something to do : the Peter Cundill investment approach / Christopher Risso-Gill.

Includes index.
ISBN 978-0-7735-3537-4
1. Cundill, Peter. 2. Value investing.
3. Securities. I. Title.

HG4521.R58 2011 332.6 C2010-907157-3

This book was designed and typeset by studio oneonone in Sabon 11/16.5

Frontispiece: Peter at base camp on the 1989 Everest expedition

Contents

Foreword
Prem Watsa

CHRISTOPHER RISSO-GILL has written this wonderful book on Peter Cundill, my friend of thirty years, which I recommend highly. Like Warren Buffett and John Templeton, Peter Cundill was a legendary practitioner of the "Value Approach according to Ben Graham."

Like many "value" investors, Pete's "road to Damascus" occurred in late 1973 when he came upon *Security Analysis* written by Ben Graham (the same thing happened to me a year later, in 1974). Fully charged, Pete took control of the All-Canadian Venture Fund in 1975 – a value investor's dream – which had fallen from $6.00 per share in 1969 to $2.00 in 1974. Changing the name to Cundill Value Fund, he went on to establish one of the best long term investment records in the business – a track record of 15.2% per annum compounded over the next thirty-three years! An investor who invested $10,000 in this fund in 1974 and kept it there was worth more than $1 million in 2007 – an increase of more than 100 times! Of course, this success resulted in the Cundill Funds growing from $8 million in 1974 to nearly $20 billion when Mackenzie Financial purchased the management company in 2006. Peter popularized the concept of "Buying a dollar for 40 cents" – which is still the slogan of the Cundill Value Fund.

Pete was always a sporting and fitness enthusiast although it was not until he was thirty-eight years old that he ran his first marathon – Buffalo to Niagara Falls. He was hooked after that, completing another twenty-two marathons over the years, all over the world.

Fortunately for us – and for Christopher Risso-Gill – Peter Cundill kept a daily journal for forty-five years. Chris's book reminds us why the investment business is so fascinating: it's always changing and there's always something to do! True to his value investment philosophy, Pete's first investment was Bethlehem Copper, a company with no debt which he bought for less than cash per share, thereby getting a producing copper mine for free. Within four months, the stock doubled and he was on his way. He then purchased Credit Foncier, which had a liquidation value of $150 per share, for $43 per share. He sold it at a multiple of his cost and the long term value investment philosophy was firmly ingrained in his mind.

True to form, Pete never bought a share of Fairfax for its first fifteen years – because it was too expensive! However, when we hit an air pocket, he loaded up on Fairfax and now has been a long term shareholder for the past ten years. We have benefitted greatly from his wisdom.

In 2001, Peter Cundill was presented with the Analysts' Choice Career Achievement Award as the greatest mutual fund manager of all time. During the ceremony, Pete was characterized as the Indiana Jones of fund managers – which he quite liked! More significantly, he was recognized as follows: "Peter Cundill has excelled as few of us can imagine and influenced a generation of investment managers while at the same time creating wealth for his investors."

In 2006, Pete was diagnosed with Fragile X, a degenerative neurological disorder. Unlike most, he took it in stride. He never moped, he founded the Cundill History Prize at McGill University, his alma mater, and he continued, as he had always done, to live his life passionately and to help others in their lives. He has always had a certain gleam in his eye when talking about investments. As Kipling said in his poem "If," Pete has always "filled the unforgiving minute with sixty seconds worth of distance run."

On 16 September 2010, we had a dinner for Pete to celebrate his life's accomplishments. The best and the brightest from the Ben Graham value school of investment attended the dinner, including Charles Brandes, Michael Price, David Winters, and the Cundill team, now led by Andy Massie and Lawrence Chin, both able successors to Pete. It was a fitting tribute to Peter Cundill's achievements. He inspired us over the past thirty-five years with his investment acumen and since 2007 he has also inspired us with his courage and determination to handle whatever cards were dealt him.

I know you will enjoy reading this book.

PREM WATSA
Toronto, 2010

THERE'S ALWAYS SOMETHING TO DO

"There's always something to do. You just need to look harder, be creative and a little flexible."

Irving Kahn

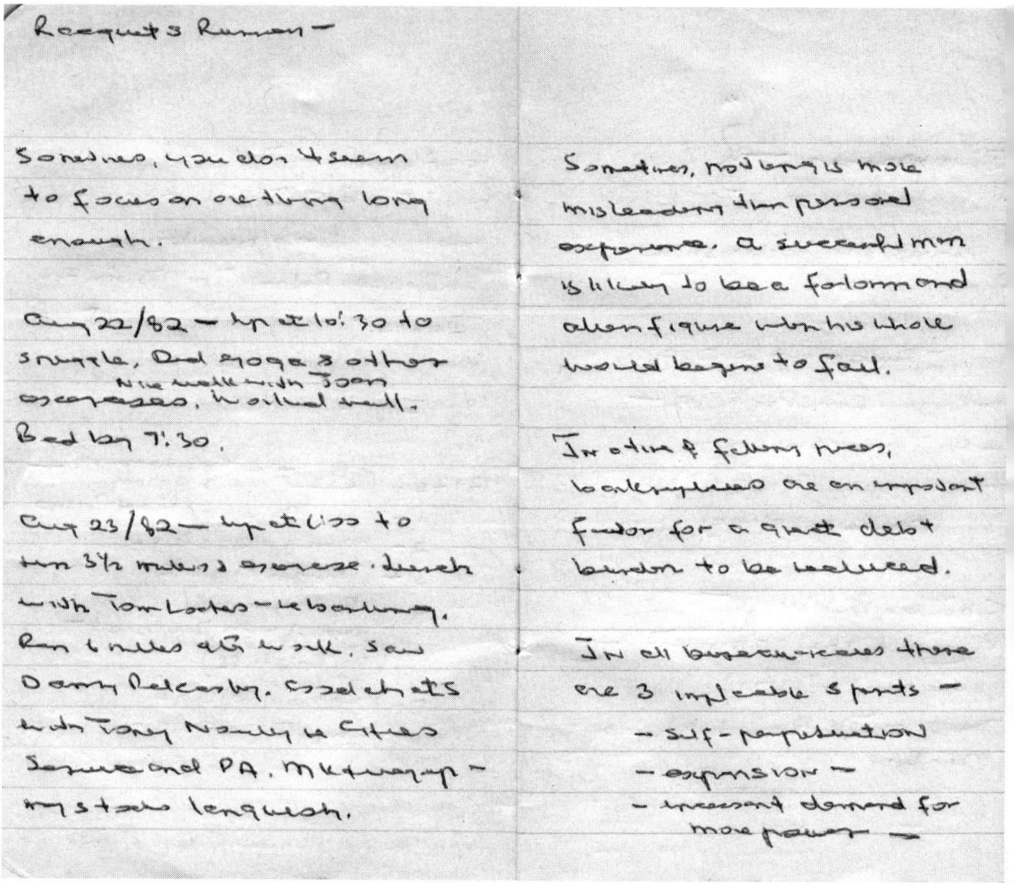
Requests Rumors —

Sometimes, you don't seem to focus on one thing long enough.

Aug 22/82 — Up at 10:30 to snuggle, and yoga & other exercises. Walked well. Nice walk with Joan.
Bed by 7:30.

Aug 23/82 — Up at 6:30 to run 3½ miles & exercise. Lunch with Tom [illegible] — [illegible].
Ran 6 miles after work, saw [illegible]. Good chats with Tony [illegible] [illegible] Square and PA. [illegible] — [illegible] language.

Sometimes, nothing is more misleading than personal experience. A successful man is likely to be a forlorn and alien figure when his whole world begins to fail.

In other & falling ways, bankruptcies are an important factor for a great debt burden to be reduced.

In all bureaucracies there are 3 implacable spirits —
— self-perpetuation
— expansion —
— incessant demand for more power —

A page from Peter's daily journals, 1963–2007. There are well over 200 of these handwritten books.

1

The Eureka Moment

ONE EVENING IN DECEMBER 1973 Peter Cundill boarded a flight from Toronto to Vancouver to return home for Christmas. He was nursing a monumental hangover and plagued by a growing sense of frustration that, having reached the mature age of thirty-five and accumulated considerable business and investment experience, all his efforts to come up with a satisfactory formula that would identify undervalued shares in the stock market with a reasonable degree of safety and consistency seemed to have led him down a series of blind alleys.

By chance he happened to be clutching a copy of *Super Money* by George Goodman; the book had been pressed into his hand by a colleague just as he was leaving the AGF Management office in downtown Toronto and, as he settled into the flight, he began rather idly to leaf through it. Within minutes his attention was riveted and he could barely contain his excitement. That night he wrote in his journal:

> Goodman devotes chapter 3 to Benjamin Graham and Warren Buffett and "the margin of safety." It struck me like a thunderbolt – there before me in plain terms was the method, the solid theoretical back-up to selecting investments based on the principle of realizable underlying value. My years of

apprenticeship are over: "THIS IS WHAT I WANT TO DO FOR THE REST OF MY LIFE!"

Peter refers to this as his moment of "epiphany" and so in many ways it has turned out to be.

What was revelatory in this chapter was surprisingly simple. A share is cheap not because it has a low price earnings multiple, a juicy dividend yield, or a very high growth rate, all of which may often be desirable, but because analysis of the balance sheet reveals that its stock market price is below its liquidation value: its intrinsic worth as a business. This above all is what constitutes "the margin of safety."

It would, however, be wrong to think that at this point Peter was in any sense an investment debutant; he rightly came to regard the entire period that preceded the epiphany moment – when the penny, so to speak, dropped – as a learning curve involving a great deal of hard labour acquiring the skills which make it possible to read a balance sheet with real understanding and a forensic attention to detail. These, of course, are the tools of the profession, but what seems to be common to nearly all the great investors is an attitude of mind that in some measure derives from family background and circumstance.

In Peter Cundill's case there were some distinctly unusual features. The family originally hailed from Yorkshire in the north of England, where they had lived for many generations as prosperous tenant farmers until they became impoverished by the long decline in agricultural prices that followed the end of the Napoleonic wars in 1815 and the gradual landlord encroachment that was a feature of the industrial revolution in England.

The result was that Peter's great-grandfather arrived in Montreal in the early 1860s with little more than a sound education and good commercial instincts, but determined to escape the poverty trap that had engulfed his family in the "old world."

He succeeded remarkably quickly, building up a very successful business importing goods from Britain to supply the needs of the fast-growing Canadian economy and the tastes of the increasingly well-to-do citizens of Montreal and beyond. He married well and was very soon adopted into the Anglo-Montreal establishment. His eldest son, Peter's grandfather, was initially even more successful, becoming a real "tycoon," who was known in New York City, to which he moved, as the "King of Camphor." By the time Peter's father was born in 1902, the family boasted all the trappings of substantial wealth: a large house in a fashionable part of Manhattan, a mansion on Staten Island looking across to the newly built Statue of Liberty, a seaside home in Connecticut staffed by numerous servants, and governesses and tutors for the children.

As a result Peter's father, Frank, was brought up as a young gentleman of wealth and privilege who could expect to choose the career that he would pursue without much regard for earning his bread. He chose the Navy, but by the time he had completed his cadet training his father's business was beginning to feel the effects of the discovery of synthetic camphor and he abandoned the idea of a career as a naval officer to help his father. Grandfather Cundill, however, was not familiar with the adage "always change a winning game" and he persisted as the business went into terminal decline, exhausting his capital and credit until in 1927 he was forced into bankruptcy.

The fairy tale life evaporated overnight and the family retreated to Montreal to live with great-grandmother Cundill. Although Frank was devastated, he immediately rolled up his sleeves and made his way out west to Alberta, for a time becoming a cowboy and rodeo rider, before returning to Montreal and finding a job with Kingstone Mackenzie Securities, eventually becoming a trader for them. He survived the crash of 1929, by his own admission largely because he had very little money to lose, but the memory of it and the anguish he witnessed remained with him for the rest of his days. In 1937 he bought a seat on the Montreal Stock Exchange, becoming an independent floor trader, and felt financially secure enough to marry early the following year. Peter was born that October.

By 1940, before Peter was even out of diapers, Frank had left for the war and the small family would not be fully reunited until 1946, when Peter was nearly eight years old. In the meantime money had been extremely short and mother and son had led a semi-nomadic existence, moving from the home of one relation to another; of no fixed abode. While not uncomfortable or necessarily unhappy, because most of the relations were well off and all were kindly disposed, they lacked a home they could really call their own.

Even after Frank was demobbed it was some time before the family's economic circumstances began to improve. The contrast between their standard of living and that of most of their friends and relations was readily apparent during Peter's boyhood and early adolescence.

Peter's professional preparation began with a Bachelor of Commerce degree from McGill, after which he decided that what he wanted was to embark on a career in the investment industry. In this he was probably influenced more by the example of his uncle Pete Scott, who was a partner of Wood Gundy and eventually became its chairman, than by his father. But he paid attention to Frank's remark that the investment business was a gamble and, if he were going to be a gambler, he would do well to have a professional qualification to fall back on, should the need arise. It was sound advice. Peter qualified as a chartered accountant, serving his articles at Price Waterhouse. This was to be invaluable, not because he ever practised but as his basic working tool.

2

Getting to First Base

AS SOON AS PETER qualified he joined the well-respected Montreal investment firm of Greenshields, where he formed an immediate bond with Frank Trebell, its youthful general manager, and secured a coveted place in the firm's Special Projects department. The group was in the initial stages of promoting the formation of the Mortgage Insurance Company of Canada (MICC) and as a CA, albeit newly qualified, Peter was charged with producing the projections for the business plan and then presenting them at board level to the prospective investing institutions, which included Alcan, the Bank of Nova Scotia, Air Canada, and the CN Pension fund. The fundraising was a success and resulted in Trebell taking Peter under his wing.

This was to have momentous consequences as Trebell was already planning his next move along the corporate ladder and wanted to take Peter with him. The result was a move out west to Vancouver where, through his relationship with Maurice Strong, who was then the CEO of Power Corporation, Trebell had engineered a takeover of the Yorkshire Trust Company, a mini-financial services conglomerate that was also Vancouver's oldest financial institution, founded at the end of the nineteenth century, coincidentally with Yorkshire money from the wealthy textile city of Huddersfield. Peter moved to Vancouver as Trebell's executive assistant, although in reality his role was more in the nature of business development. His focus had started to gravitate away from mortgages, fixed interest instruments, and real estate towards equities, which he now believed were likely to offer the most attractive investment returns over the long term. He was prompted to confide in his journal:

> My primary objective is to make money for my clients and then to make my business profitable. I believe that the way to achieve this is through associating with truly competent people with unshakeable business integrity, to ensure strict financial controls, a culture of thoroughness, a measured capacity for action; i.e. no seat of the pants stuff and a spirit of humility and cohesive teamwork. What I am beginning to perceive is that investors tend to follow trends and fashion rather than taking the trouble to look for value. This must offer opportunity for the professional investment manager, as a result of the short term mispricing of securities.

During his early days at Yorkshire Peter wrote and passed the Chartered Financial Analyst Association exams as part of one of the first groups to qualify. The work involved elicited another important comment.

> I think that intelligent forecasting (company revenues, earnings, etc.) should not seek to predict what will in fact happen in the future. Its purpose ought to be to illuminate the road, to point out obstacles and potential pitfalls and so assist management to tailor events and to bend them in a desired direction. Forecasting should be used as a device to put both problems and opportunities into perspective. It is a management tool, but it

can never be a substitute for strategy, nor should it ever be used as the primary basis for portfolio investment decisions.

One can see that, almost by default, Peter was even then veering toward a value approach and in fact his first major equity investment exhibits most of the characteristics that are associated with a value-based purchase. Peter was already looking out for solid companies in unfashionable industries whose shares had fallen sharply and Bethlehem Copper came to his attention. In the absence of negative corporate news justifying the price decline, he suspected that the shares might be cheap. Quite how cheap they were did not become clear until he had subjected the company to his own brand of exhaustive analysis, which made it apparent that the shares were trading at the price of the cash on the company's balance sheet, on top of which it had no debt and owned a profitable producing mine with solid long-term contracts for the purchase of its copper production. Peter quietly built up a significant position in Bethlehem for clients of the Yorkshire at an average cost of around $4.50 per share.

Both Bethlehem and mining stocks in general were totally out of favour with the investing public at the time. However in Peter's developing judgement this was not just an irrelevance but a positive bonus. He had inadvertently stumbled upon a classic net-net: a company whose share price was trading below its working capital, net all its liabilities. It was the first such discovery of his career and had the additional merit of proving the efficacy of value theory almost immediately, had he been able to recognize it as such. Within four months Bethlehem had doubled and in six months he was able to start selling some of the position at $13.00. The overall impact on portfolio performance had been dramatic.

In later years Peter became well known as an inveterate traveller who would routinely clock up well over a hundred thousand miles a year in the quest for bargains in international markets and especially for his habit of making a special effort to visit whichever country had had the worst performing stock market in the previous eleven months. His professional curiosity was boundless, but it was far from being confined only to strictly professional matters. Peter's approach had much in common with that of the old style merchant banker, who believed it was as important to sniff the air and gauge the commercial temperature as it was to examine the numbers. He always felt that an understanding of local politics and the culture and character of the people was an important factor in inspiring enough confidence to make investments in unfashionable and even positively outlandish locations and, even when the numbers might appear compelling, if he became uncomfortable with the "feel" of a place, he would pass on an investment.

Peter made his first visit to Japan in March 1969 and his immediate impressions are worth quoting in full, not just because Japan was to become such an important factor in his investment success but for the insight they offer into the entirely open-minded way in which he habitually engaged with whatever new territory he might be exploring. The visit had been organized by his friend Yuge-san, an executive with Nippon Steel who had become a good friend in Vancouver over many late evenings and much sake and gin.

> My first impression of Tokyo was of a busy, bustling, construction crazy city, glazed and diffused through an orange sky. Snow is still very much in evidence with the temperature in the mid 40s. The Otari hotel has over 1000 rooms and a sushi restaurant. Yuge-san took me for drinks and dinner in the Chinese restaurant in the basement – absolutely first class – and then downtown for a steam bath; relaxing even when the masseuse was walking on me. As Yuge-san observed it was

> a pure steam bath, like a Turkish bath, not what he called an "obscene" one. He suggested that we might have an "obscene" one later in the week! I was struck by the contrast between the frenetic movement all around me and the stillness of the people's quiet courtesy – also by the Western influence evident everywhere, which I had not quite expected. I am in no doubt *this is a major economic power*!

The visit included a formal tea in the oldest part of Tokyo with Yuge-san's mother and sister, exquisitely dressed in beautiful kimonos, and dinner at home with his wife and two small children, as well as a formal meeting with the Nippon finance team. In the course of the week Peter had felt able to ask a number of the sort of questions that would be considered completely inappropriate in Western society. He established that Yuge-san earned 300 yen per month; far from a fortune despite being quite senior. Once the rent on the Nippon apartment and the lease on the car had been paid there was not a great deal left over for anything else. The family's entertainment, as well as any of the very brief holidays that there might be, were Nippon organized and sponsored as a kind of family corporate activity. Peter drew some interesting conclusions from the information.

> This is clearly still a paternalistic society which, despite war and industrialization on a vast scale, retains many quite feudal characteristics.
>
> The conditions of employment actually go a long way towards explaining how it is possible for Japanese industry to be so price competitive. It enables the cost of labour to be strictly controlled and kept at minimum levels, while at the same time corporate loyalty is very carefully nurtured by fostering the idea that the corporation itself, with all of its employees,

their wives and their children, represents a kind of extended family, or clan, with all of the old fashioned obligations that this implies in both directions. I get no feeling that there is the slightest undercurrent of discontent lurking, so it seems possible to imagine that this personnel culture still has plenty of life left in it, despite the abundant evidence of western influence in Japanese consumer culture.

This trip [which had included Hong Kong and Thailand] has given me a whole new set of perspectives. I now see Canada as really tiny, although affluent. If these mainland Asian countries, and especially China, were ever to get their act together economically like Japan they could rival the whole of North America and the rest of the developed world without even blinking. There have to be investment opportunities both in Japan and in mainland China – perhaps through Hong Kong.

The next significant step that Peter took with portfolio investment was to buy into a most unusual equity that, as it were, fell into his lap. In 1970 Maurice Strong had left Power Corporation to work for the Canadian Government and corporate enthusiasm for their investment in the Yorkshire Trust had departed with him. Placing the Power Corporation's shares did not prove to be difficult. One of the Yorkshire's new shareholders turned out to be a curious sort of hybrid known as Credit Foncier Franco Canadien. In his habitually thorough fashion Peter took the trouble to scrutinize the Credit Foncier annual report in considerable detail. What he discovered was intensely exciting. The company was, as he described it, "a treasure trove of wonderful assets."

It had been founded towards the end of the nineteenth century by the powerful French banking group Compagnie Financière de Paris et des Pays Bas, colloquially known as Paribas, with the idea of entering the mortgage lending market in Quebec and the Maritimes and had been encouraged to make loans with a more entrepreneurial, risk-taking approach than the Canadian Chartered Banks. As a result it had become a key player in the Prairie provinces just at the time that those vast areas, hitherto the untamed domain of the buffalo herds and the Plains Indians, were gradually being converted into one of the world's greatest grain-producing expanses. Credit Foncier had been substantially involved in financing pioneer farmers and had done extremely well out of the enterprise: the profits had enabled it to acquire a significant commercial real estate portfolio in the fast growing cities of eastern Canada.

When the depression struck at the end of the 1920s, Credit Foncier foreclosed on many of the farmers, who had been unable to keep up with their mortgage payments, but in doing so it followed an unusually enlightened policy, allowing the farmers to remain as tenants on very favourable rental terms rather than insisting on an eviction followed by a fire-sale. Many had opted for this tenancy deal and Credit Foncier had thereby become the owner of swathes of farmland, including the underlying mineral rights, and whenever the land had been sold, they had kept those rights. By the early 1970s, as commodity prices, including oil, began to rise, the company, somewhat unexpectedly, found itself sitting on a very considerable portfolio of highly prospective mineral wealth. As well, as Peter immediately saw, their accounting policies had remained ultra conservative, with the entire real estate portfolio carried on the balance sheet at book cost with no attempt to put a realistic value on the mineral rights.

Credit Foncier's corporate structure was also most unusual. Although Paribas was the controlling shareholder, the shares of the Canadian entity were listed in Montreal and Paris and there was a float of about 30%, the majority of which was held by institutions in

Paris, especially by some of the more exclusive private banks. There were two boards, a Canadian board of directors, which ran the Canadian operation, and a French board, whose members had the unusual entitlement of benefitting as individuals from 20% of the profits generated in Canada.

Naturally enough there was a good deal of competition at senior management level within Paribas to secure a seat on the Credit Foncier board and this privilege had come to be regarded as a special reward for particularly valuable service and sometimes as a retirement perk. But times were changing and the Canadian board members were becoming restive over this arcane and unconventional structure, which did not sit entirely comfortably with prevailing Canadian corporate practice. To Peter it seemed like a license to loot the candy store: neither the cash nor the real value of the assets was even remotely adequately reflected in the share price and, given the tension that was beginning to emerge between the two boards, it was not hard to envisage that in the foreseeable future there might be a clash that could act as a catalyst to draw public attention to the underlying value or perhaps eventually precipitate an outright disposal by Paribas, which would immediately unlock shareholder value. The more that he looked, the more perfect the opportunity revealed itself to be: Credit Foncier ticked all the boxes, having been consistently profitable and paying dividends for many years.

A reasonable estimate of liquidation value appeared to be in excess of $150 per share. Within days Peter began quietly to accumulate a position at around $43 per share. For Canada the discount was undoubtedly extreme, although, as Peter was to discover when some years later he began buying shares in Europe, luckily it was not quite so uncommon in those markets. Peter found the Credit Foncier experience totally engrossing and from that point onward was completely captivated by the thrill of making an investment discovery. He confided in his journal:

> I believe that there is probably one opportunity in every man's life which demands his knowledge, his guts, his self-esteem, and his judgement. If he seizes it with both hands and it is successful, he joins the first rank, if not he remains a mortal with feet of clay. Credit Foncier may well be my test.

Shortly after writing this Peter went to a dinner at the Vancouver Club attended by Yorkshire Trust clients and some of the City's most substantial investors; he outlined the Credit Foncier story and added a thumbnail sketch of his view of corporate conditions in France:

> I told them that the French corporate world had been shaken to its core eighteen months ago by the first hostile takeover bid in its history and that this was an indication that self-serving management and contempt for shareholders were in their death throes in the Gallic world, which could well be good news for CFFC. I don't think anyone was listening.

Peter was in fact mistaken in that supposition. The group had not forgotten that he had identified the unnoticed opportunity in Bethlehem Copper. It was becoming apparent that Peter was not just some run of the mill broker punting an unusual, but probably poorly researched, idea in order to differentiate himself from the pack. So the story began to percolate and within two months the share price of Credit Foncier had risen almost imperceptibly by 25%.

As far as Peter was concerned this was merely the beginning of what he foresaw as a wonderful ride and he was never an investor who was easily tempted to sell before the underlying value of a security had been unlocked, merely to realize a quick flip. Within a few months Peter's informal syndicate controlled over 2% of the Credit Foncier equity capital, making it the Canadian company's second largest shareholder. The list of the investors who made up the group was impressive: Canadian Forest Products, another of the Yorkshire shareholders; Greenshields and Wood Gundy; Cemp, the investment vehicle of the Bronfman family; and American General Funds. By then the shares had risen to $65 and the group was continuing to buy.

3

Launching a Mutual Fund on Value Principles

BY THE BEGINNING OF THE 1970S Peter's relationship with Frank Trebell had deteriorated to the point where he felt his position at Yorkshire had become untenable. He suspected that as a director he was not being kept fully informed and he was increasingly doubtful about Trebell's effectiveness as chief executive. In his view the opportunity to build on the Yorkshire's solid reputation and turn a sleepy but sound institution into the premier financial services group in western Canada had been squandered in a series of ill-conceived expansionary moves, which had been inadequately planned and resourced and poorly executed. His unease and frustration emerge very clearly in his journal:

> I hate people who are imprecise and even more those who are opaque or quite deliberately evasive; they just create mayhem and disaster in the world around them. I do believe in change and that an element of risk-taking is a necessary adjunct of growing any successful business, but it has to be measured and controlled and its extent clearly understood. I do not advocate complacency, but I am conservative by nature. I am not a real estate developer and I am not prepared to take those sorts of

risks. I am afraid that the Trust Company will suffer if this continues. It will be starved of capital and exposed to bad decisions made in the Yorkshire Finance Corp., with the consequent loss of credibility, which is the corner-stone of what we have to sell.

Peter severed the cord with Trebell. In September 1971 his friend Warren Goldring persuaded him to open a representative office for AGF Management Limited in Vancouver as an investment counsellor. His decision was well timed, since a few months later Trebell was reported to the BC Securities Commission in connection with some irregularities in a real estate transaction and simultaneously to the Ontario Securities Commission over back pricing in a group of mutual funds that was managed and operated out of Toronto. He was eventually arrested, tried, and sent to prison.

Peter was asked to assist in both investigations and did so without rancour but with complete candour, and eventually had to testify for the prosecution at the trial. As he recorded, it was an awful task:

> It is awesome how a single character flaw, in this case an overwhelming capacity to obliterate inconvenient facts, has led to complete self-destruction. Frank has so many admirable qualities but that flaw in combination with a certain degree of sloppiness and imperfect integrity have simply eaten away at an otherwise fine man. As a result of all this I have become even more acutely aware of the vital importance of good housekeeping, attention to detail, and the dangers of self delusion.

Notwithstanding this difficult experience, Peter had not been deflected from his quest for the "holy grail" of consistency, risk control, and predictability in portfolio investment. On the basis of his investment selection of Bethlehem Copper and Credit Foncier it might have been perfectly fair to conclude that he was just a "natural" value investor, but this would be to oversimplify and to ignore the fact that Peter was and is an investment theoretician and philosopher. Those two first outstanding selections were indeed classic value plays. However, Peter had not based his decisions on discernable and repeatable principles; as yet he had no solid theoretical grounding that could provide a consistent methodology, or analytical tool, for the construction of a complete and uniformly conceived investment portfolio.

Not that he had neglected to explore all kinds of investment theories. In fact, in his search he had come to two important conclusions: that the majority of models used by investment research departments were essentially worthless and that attempting to make general market calls was a "mug's game." Most of the analytical tools tended to be heavily reliant on extrapolating history and market calls involved far too many variables, as well as being conditioned by the herd instinct, which, more often than not, was triggered by some completely unpredictable event. He also concluded that pure chartists were simple fantasists, in approximately the same category as those gambling punters who believe that they can predict the next fall of a roulette ball on the basis of previous history. Despite all his efforts, although he had recorded some useful thoughts that seemed to be leading him in the right kind of direction, up to the moment when he read *Super Money* on the airplane a satisfactory, comprehensive answer had eluded him. As his summary at this time shows, he had not really made great progress, except perhaps through the elimination of many of the "dead ends":

- Management's ability to predict earnings is universally poor.
- It is the strategic modelling behind a portfolio that matters most.
- One needs to develop a sense of spaced maturities in a

common stock portfolio in a way that is comparable to a bond portfolio.
- In a macro sense it may be more useful to spend time analysing industries instead of national or international economies.
- It must be essential to develop and specify a precise investment policy that investors can understand and rely on the portfolio manager to implement.

When Peter had first joined AGF, Allan Manford, the chair, had given him a book called *Institutional Investing* by Charles Ellis, in which the author suggested that any money manager worth his salt ought to be able to achieve a 35% compound annual rate of return. Quite obviously this was not something that was happening at AGF, or indeed being achieved by any other money manager with whom Peter was familiar, but he was hypnotized by the statement. It was clear to him that both Bethlehem and Credit Foncier had individually more than achieved this benchmark and he began to try to determine some of the common characteristics that had led to this success and might make it possible to duplicate these choices.

He started his investigation by subjecting the two securities to a form of regression analysis that he had devised for the purpose, the idea being to arrive at a "predicted judgement of likely price appreciation." The departure point was to define what he considered to be the most important variables and give each of them a weighting that he could adjust later in light of the outcome. This approach was valid because he already knew what the actual price appreciation had been over any given period, once the first investment had been made. The categories of variable that he chose were book value, dividend growth, growth in earnings per share, frequency of senior management changes/philosophy, favourable/unfavourable industry environment, degree of recognition by the investment public, general economic environment, available float, flow of funds, general level of interest rates, equivalent money instruments, time horizon, and the feel of the company.

The equation was $\text{Appa} = \text{Jppa} - (V1+V2+V3\ldots)$ where Appa is the actual percentage price appreciation, Jppa the anticipated percentage price appreciation, and V is the weighted variable. Of course it was far too complicated to work satisfactorily. It needed the combined wisdom of Ben Graham and Warren Buffett for Peter to make his breakthrough and the moment could not have been more opportune.

One positive aspect of the "fall out" from the Yorkshire affair was that the All Canadian group of funds that had been a victim of the "back pricing" activity came up for sale. As the news had spread and the scale of the misdemeanours had been publicized and amplified in the financial press, the level of redemptions in these funds had grown from a trickle to a tidal wave, with the result that the management contracts for the individual funds were up for sale at knock down prices.

As luck would have it, Peter was already familiar with one of the funds: the All Canadian Venture Fund. This fund had been issued to the public in early 1967 at which time it had had assets of $14 million with a unit price of $4.30. During the bull market of 1967–69 the assets had risen to $50 million and the unit price to $6.00. The fund's original investment policy had been to invest in the high growth sectors of the economy with particular emphasis on developing technology. The market break in 1970 had hit funds of this kind especially hard because bear markets have a tendency to penalize concept investments in favour of established businesses with earnings. Redemptions, on top of the decline in the value of the portfolio, had reduced the fund to its original asset levels and the unit price had slumped. The manager's response was to change investment tack in favour of the latest fad in the natural resource and energy sector. Once more all went well at the outset, but the market turned sour again and by the end of 1974 the unit price had slumped for the second time to just over $2.00 and assets in the fund, in the wake of the scandal, stood at just over $7 million.

By this time redemptions had slowed to a trickle again; the remaining investors, either shell-shocked or punch drunk, had presumably pushed their certificates to the back of a drawer and were binning the quarterly reports. For Peter this was the opportunity and in some respects it was similar to a value investment. He had finally managed to sell his shares in the Yorkshire for $100,000. This was a far cry from the $400,000 valuation of the year before, but it was sufficient for Peter, with Gowan Guest, a Vancouver lawyer whom he had met through Tory party politics, as his partner, to buy the management contract of the All Canadian Venture Fund.

The months preceding the acquisition had been far from idle in terms of the development of Peter's investment thinking. He had devoured Graham and Dodd's *Security Analysis*, especially chapter 41 entitled "The Asset-Value Factor in Common-Stock Valuation," which in his copy is heavily underlined and liberally annotated. He wasted no time in writing to the long-suffering All Canadian unitholders signalling yet another change of policy and he made a compelling case. It was quite a letter:

> It seems to me that a new strategy has to be found. Investment in emerging companies whose activities are orientated towards new technologies is better suited to corporations who themselves specialize in that area. In addition it is my view that it may take twenty or thirty years, a new set of analysts, and a new generation of market players before stock markets react to these types of security as they did in the mid to late 60s.

I would like to suggest a new concept that will offer shareholders an opportunity to realize significant and steady capital appreciation. It is not a new idea in that it is essentially a "return to value" philosophy pioneered by the dean of analysts, Professor Benjamin Graham, and his successor Warren Buffett. For a twenty-year period up to 1955, Graham, through his Graham-Newman fund, averaged more than 20% growth per annum using the techniques that I shall outline below. Warren Buffett managed to achieve a 30% growth rate for his shareholders, turning $100,000 into $100 million between 1956 and 1969 when he returned the money to his stockholders because he could find no more bargains in the market. He returned to the investment market in November 1974.

The essential concept is to buy under-valued, unrecognized, neglected, out of fashion, or misunderstood situations where inherent value, a margin of safety, and the possibility of sharply changing conditions created new and favourable investment opportunities. Although a large number of holdings might be held, performance was invariably established by concentrating in a few holdings. In essence, the fund invested in companies that, as a result of detailed fundamental analysis, were trading below their "intrinsic value." The intrinsic value was defined as the price that a private investor would be prepared to pay for the security if it were not listed on a public stock exchange. The analysis was based as much on the balance sheet as it was on the statement of profit and loss.

Based on my studies and experience, investments for the Venture Fund should only be made if most of the following criteria are met:

- The share price must be less than book value. Preferably

it will be less than net working capital less long term debt.

- The price must be less than one half of the former high and preferably at or near its all time low.
- The price earning multiple must be less than ten or the inverse of the long term corporate bond rate, whichever is the less.
- The company must be profitable. Preferably it will have increased its earnings for the past five years and there will have been no deficits over that period.
- The company must be paying dividends. Preferably the dividend will have been increasing and have been paid for some time.
- Long term debt and bank debt (including off-balance sheet financing) must be judiciously employed. There must be room to expand the debt position if required.

In addition, studies should be made of past and expected future rates of profitability, the ability of the management, and the various underlying factors and hypotheses that govern sales volume, costs, and profit after taxes. Of course, one should never become an absolute slave to the above criteria, but they have proved to my satisfaction to be a vital starting point.

My own exposure to this type of investment procedure has been as follows: On January 1st 1973, we started with $600,000 and, utilizing these techniques, the unit value appreciated by 35.2%. During the same period the All Canadian Venture Fund was down by 49%, the TSE industrials by 20%, and the Dow Jones Industrial Index by 26%.

To the best of my knowledge, this investment philosophy would have outperformed every mutual fund in Canada over this period. This fund never owned more than ten stocks and

50% of its assets were at one time concentrated in just two stocks (Bethlehem Copper and Credit Foncier).

Privately he confided some of his other investment principles to the journal and they too make fascinating reading:

> I will never use inside information or seek it out. I do implicitly believe in Sir Sigmund Warburg's adage, "All you get from inside information is a whiff of bad breath." In fact it is worse than that because it can actually paralyse reasoning powers; imperilling the cold detached judgement required so that the hard facts can shape decisions. Intuition, whether positive or negative, is quite another matter. It is a vital component of my art.
>
> Stock manipulations only have a limited and temporary effect on markets. In the end it is always the economic facts and the values which are the determining factors. Actually value in an investment is similar to character in an individual – it stands up better in adversity which it overcomes more readily.
>
> Once the analysis is complete and you have reached the firm conviction that an investment is right you should not try to be too clever about the purchase price. If you have to take a loss do it decisively – don't dither. Learn the lessons and then forget about it.
>
> In every analysis you need to isolate what the real assets are and you must not forget to examine the franchise to do business, to review the *character and competence* of the management and to estimate the outcome if the whole business had to be turned into cash.

Some of these thoughts, which relate to the overriding Benjamin Graham principle of the margin of safety, were the fruit of a ripening relationship with Irving Kahn, one of the doyens of value investment, who in some ways became the mentor to Peter that Trebell had failed in the end to be. In a very real sense spending time with Irving and becoming immersed in his investment thinking was tantamount to sitting at the feet of Ben Graham – the master himself – since Irving's own apprenticeship had been as Graham's teaching assistant at the Columbia Business School. Irving was also a founder member of the New York Society of Securities Analysts and one of the first to become a chartered financial analyst. Today, at the age of a hundred and five, he continues to work, often on week-ends as well, remarking recently that one of the beauties of his profession is that there is no mandatory retirement age and at this stage in his life he can still get pleasure out of finding a cheap stock. Irving and his son Alan, who followed in his footsteps, have been and remain some of Peter's most steadfast friends and supporters.

There was another principle, not directly related to investment, that had also begun to take shape in Peter's mind. Exercise and fitness had long been a fixed feature of his routines, though they had never taken on the dimensions of an endurance test or an outright challenge. Through his extracurricular reading Peter had been absorbing some of the athletic ideals of ancient Greece, which broadly propound the theory that athletic stamina and mental resilience go hand in hand. The legendary feat of Pheidippides' 240 kilometre run from Athens to Sparta and back, or the alternative version of his run to Athens, straight from the battlefield at Marathon, to deliver the news of the Greek victory over the Persians, had sparked Peter's imagination and the idea of running a marathon began to intrigue him and he decided to attempt it. Fortunately he was already extremely fit because he left himself a bare six weeks to prepare for the Buffalo to Niagara Falls Marathon in the fall of 1976. Peter was just about to turn thirty-eight and had never run more than five miles before he began his training, but he had built up to a distance of twenty miles just before the event.

A week after his final training run, on a cold cloudy morning, he found himself driving from Toronto to Buffalo dressed in his running shorts. He found the first twenty-one miles relatively easy, running along the river towards the Falls, although they never seemed to get any closer. From miles fifteen to twenty-one he was running with fluid confidence, as though in a trance, passing lots of other runners and wondering somewhat complacently what all the fuss was about. But then he hit the fabled wall and found that his legs suddenly had no punch and were not responding, so that it was will-power alone that kept him going through the last five miles. Even then he only just made it to the finishing line, collapsing into a friend's arms, eyes glazed, sugar depleted, dehydrated, and suffering from loss of balance. He now understood intuitively what it was that would have killed Pheidippides; twenty-six miles on a cool, wettish morning was hard enough, but running across the burning plain of Marathon in early September, almost certainly without any water, would undoubtedly have been fatal. Peter's time was a very respectable 3.13 and he could simply have notched up the achievement and left it at that, but the psychology of the race had gripped him, as had the mental tenacity that he had needed to call upon to complete it, and he was hooked for good, running another twenty-two races over the years.

As Peter had perhaps anticipated, there was no reaction whatsoever from the All Canadian Venture Fund shareholders to his letter setting out the proposed changes in the fund's investment policy. However, all that was required to proceed with it was board approval. Peter had already decided that the new value approach would be better served and more smoothly implemented with a new board of directors, which was to be made up of people with whom he had a strong rapport, who had had first-hand experience of his stock picking abilities, and who understood the principles of value investment.

In addition to his partner Gowan Guest, who became chair, he chose Peter Webster, a member of the wealthy Quebec family that had owned the Toronto *Globe and Mail* and a friend as well as a Yorkshire Trust investment client; his oldest friend Michael Meighen, later to become a senator; John McLernon, a friend from McGill days who had become a very young and dynamic president of Macaulay Nicolls Maitland; and Hugh Snyder, the president of Western Mining, a convinced admirer of Peter's investment skills, particularly since the success of the investment in Bethlehem Copper. As part of the new broom approach Peter also changed the name from the All Canadian Venture Fund to the Cundill Value Fund and enshrined his own take on the Benjamin Graham investment criteria in the minutes of the first meeting of the new board.

As soon as all the administrative details were properly in place, Peter wasted no time. His research notebooks were already crammed with investigative security analysis, amongst which some outstanding investment opportunities were lurking. However, the share that was to have the most significant, immediate effect on the new Value Fund was, at first glance, a most unlikely contender. For this reason it is a perfect illustration of the versatility with which value principles can be applied to any security, anywhere, in any industry.

By the beginning of 1976 the world-wide recession had bitten hard and, as is usually the case when economic conditions are causing general corporate stress, the advertising industry had been hurt more than most, with very sharply falling revenues, much publicized redundancies, and gloomy predictions that the market would never fully recover and margins would consequently continue to be squeezed for years to come. As a result J. Walter Thompson (JWT), a household name in the industry, had no stock market friends at all. It had gone public in 1972 at over $20.00 per share and was now trading at $4.00. Both institutional and retail investors were completely disillusioned and there was the added negative that H.R. Haldeman, President Nixon's ex-chief of staff, who had previously been the head of JWT's large Los Angeles office, had recently been imprisoned for his part in the Watergate conspiracy.

However, as the shares at $4.00 were trading at less than 20% of their previous high, the company had caught Peter's attention and he had ordered the annual report and the 10K. What he discovered sent prickles up his spine: the company had a hard book value of $18.00 per share, not including its freehold buildings in Paris and Tokyo, and it had a long-term lease in Berkeley Square at the heart of London's Mayfair. This was not all – it was still profitable and was paying a dividend. Peter began buying at once and carried steadily on up to his limit of 10% of the assets of the fund. The average cost was just over $8.00 per share.

During the course of his buying program Peter visited the company several times and on one visit was asked if he would step aside to have a word with the president, Don Johnston. Johnston came straight to the point, "What do you know that we don't? We're selling stock from the pension fund and you're buying?! Who's behind this?"

Peter's reply was nothing if not frank, "I'm buying your stock because it's cheap and for no other reason. But you may not be aware that if there were an acquirer and he got control at anywhere near this price ($11.00), he would be able to liquidate your company at a very substantial profit and I'm placing no value on the name, although that must also be worth something."

Johnston merely looked confused and wished Peter well. He was an advertising man and a good one, but financially naïve. However, some months later Sam Belzberg's First City Financial filed a 13D, a statutory public document required by the Securities and Exchange Commission as soon as any single shareholder's interest exceeds 5% of a company's equity capital, effectively putting JWT into play as a takeover candidate. How Belzberg got to hear of it remains something of a mystery, but Peter sold his stock a year later for well over $20.00 per share.

The results of Peter's stewardship of his own fund were nothing short of spectacular and are set out in the 1977 annual report as follows:

	Cundill Value Fund	DJII	TSEII
1975	+32%	+39%	+10%
1976	+32%	+17%	+6%
1977	+21%	-21%	+6%

However, this success had generated its own problem, which is referred to in the annual report of the fund:

> Although during the last three years our investments have increased in value by approximately $1.5 million per annum, we have been suffering annual redemptions of about the same amount.

This is, of course, a typical knee-jerk reaction: many of the tired old investors are only too delighted to clamber out at the first signs of a recovery and a second wave of selling frequently occurs as soon as issue price or historic purchase price are attained once more. In this limbo situation the rest of the world has either not yet noticed the performance numbers or doubts their sustainability. For Peter this was intensely frustrating, especially as his fledgling fund had very limited resources to devote to any kind of marketing program and his own efforts, single-handed, were simply not enough to generate a wave of new interest. Serendipity was, however, about to come to the rescue, aided by Peter's personal credentials in coming from solid Yorkshire stock.

The founding shareholders of the Yorkshire Trust Company were a wealthy Huddersfield family by the name of Norton. In addition to their 25% interest in that company, they also owned a private holding company that had assets of about $10 million, consisting of a portfolio of marketable securities and the freehold of an office building in Vancouver. The original purpose of this vehicle had been to try to minimize the incidence of British taxation on individual family shareholders and it had worked well for three generations. However, with the advent of a fourth generation, the number of shareholders had proliferated and the fact that there was no selling mechanism, and therefore no liquidity, was becoming increasingly irksome. Simply liquidating the company would immediately have triggered a very substantial capital gains tax liability for all the shareholders, whether or not they were willing sellers. Consequently the family was looking for a tax-efficient way of resolving the problem.

Peter had impressed George Norton, the head of the family, when they had first met in Vancouver after he had joined the Yorkshire Trust, and he had also taken the trouble to visit Norton on his home ground in Huddersfield. The upshot was that a deal was struck whereby Peter issued units in the Cundill Value Fund to the various members of the Norton family in exchange for their shares in the private company. Peter then sold the building and the portfolio and more than doubled the assets of the Value Fund, at the same time solving the family's tax problem and acquiring a solid group of long-term investors.

4

Value Investment in Action

THE RECOVERY OF THE GLOBAL ECONOMY after the recession and the stock market collapse of 1973/4 was followed by a golden decade for value investment. The severity of the downturn meant that the choice of securities that qualified for investment under Peter's broad criteria was bewilderingly large, and in this respect there are some similarities with today. But the stricter standards he had chosen to apply in the balance sheet analysis of the "intrinsic value" test, which he had described as "mostly Graham, a little Buffett and a bit of Cundill," imposed their own discipline and assisted him enormously in narrowing the field of choice to manageable proportions. The result was a number of startlingly successful value discoveries that rapidly propelled the Value Fund into the premier performance league in North America.

The complete neglect in which some of the fallen darlings of the market now languished meant that it was possible to construct substantial positions without greatly disturbing the share price and this was precisely what Peter set about doing.

J. Walter Thompson was the first of the companies where Peter came to control 4.9% of the entire equity, but it was quickly followed by the American Investment Company. Founded in 1931, AIC had grown into one of the largest personal loan companies in the United

States. As was to be expected in the rather unsettled economic climate, consumer finance generally was under a cloud and shares of AIC were trading at $3.00, down from a high of over $30.00. However, there was a hard book value of over $12.00, some valuable old real estate assets that were carried at cost, and some useful tax loss carry forwards.

By then the retail loan market had recovered sufficiently for AIC to have returned to profitability and there was even some talk of a resumption of the dividend. Peter could find no flaws and immediately bought 200,000 shares at $3.00. Six months later he had accumulated over 5% and had filed a 13D with the SEC declaring his position. At the time he confided to the journal:

> As I proceed with this specialization into buying cheap securities I have reached two conclusions. Firstly, very few people really do their homework properly, so now I always check for myself. Secondly, if you have confidence in your own work, you have to take the initiative without waiting around for someone else to take the first plunge. I haven't yet found a solution for determining timing on the sell tack. People say it ought to be largely dependent on one's perception of the trend in the overall stock market, but I am suspicious of this. I think that the financial community devotes far too much time and mental resource to its constant efforts to predict the economic future and consequent stock market behaviour using a disparate, and almost certainly incomplete, set of statistical variables. It makes me wonder what might be accomplished if all this time, energy, and money were to be applied to endeavours with a better chance of proving reliable and practically useful. The timing difficulty in selling does not

lie in not knowing when the trading discount to intrinsic value has been eliminated, but in judging by how much it is likely to be surpassed.

Shortly after filing the 13D on the AIC position Peter received a call inviting him to join the board of the company. He deliberated carefully over whether to accept, concerned that the board seat would position him as an insider and restrict his freedom of action. He discussed the question with Stuart Shapiro, a bright New York attorney and subsequently a great friend, who had a reputation for getting straight to the point. Stuart's response was typically blunt; "Well, my friend, if you wanna be a real player, you gotta actually start playing."

Peter did join the board and as a result he clocked up many thousands of miles over the years making the awkward journey to the AIC headquarters in St Louis, but it was a prestigious role that brought with it some valuable associations, good merger and acquisition experience, and, probably most important of all, his meeting with Tony Novelly, the self-made owner of Apex Oil, who became one of his closest friends, a great supporter and "confidant," and a client as well.

AIC was very quickly put into play and this resulted in bids from Household Finance and Gulf and Western. Although both of these offers ran into regulatory problems and eventually fell through, AIC was taken over in the end by Leucadia at $13.00 per share, two years after Peter took his initial position. It was a perfect example of the way in which a value buyer can act effectively as a catalyst, but it had demanded a great deal of Peter's time, attention, and energy and, above all else, the exercise of patience.

The question of timing on the sell side was brought into particular focus by Peter's investment in Tiffany and Co., the iconic Fifth

Avenue jeweller and silversmith. His analysis had revealed that the stock was trading below both book and liquidation value. It had produced positive earnings since 1961 and paid dividends (occasionally out of reserves) since 1868. Notwithstanding all this, where short-term stock market performance is concerned, perception is everything and the pundits were negative about Tiffany on two counts. First, it had lost money for several years in the 1930s, when luxury goods had been neither fashionable nor generally affordable and there was a consensus that the 1970s were likely to see a repeat of this so luxury brands were definitely out of favour. Second, Tiffany's equity was controlled by Walter Hoving, its chief executive, who, although recognized as a talented and energetic manager with real creative flair, had roundly declared in public that he would never ever sell.

In fact Tiffany's profits grew steadily right through the recession of the early 70s, with revenues climbing from $23 million in 1970 to $35 million in 1974 and net income rising above the $1 million mark for the first time ever in that same year. However, in the light of subsequent events, the meaning of Hoving's use of "never" was to require some qualification.

For Peter, of course, the clincher in making an investment decision would always be the value of the net assets and in Tiffany's case there were plenty to choose from. The most obvious and high profile was the famous Tiffany Diamond, a massive 128.5 carat canary-coloured brilliant – the largest in the world – that was carried on the books for $1.00 although it was public knowledge that the company had recently turned down an offer of $2 million for it. Nevertheless, this was not the real jewel in the crown: the freehold of the Tiffany building on Fifth Avenue had sat on the books valued at $1 million since 1940. Prime Manhattan real estate had risen dramatically since that date and, recession or no recession, it was indisputably continuing to do so.

There was no goodwill in the books, so the brand was effectively valued at zero. It was obvious to Peter that if Cartier in Paris and Asprey in London were considered to be valuable as brands, the Tiffany name was unlikely to be the exception. On top of this there was a factory of 120,000 square feet in Newark and a very conservative valuation placed on the inventory of retail stock. The shares were trading below the book value of $10.50 and in Peter's judgement well below the company's realistic liquidation value, so he quietly accumulated 3% of Tiffany at an average of $8.00 per share and then went to visit Walter Hoving.

Peter was not the first predator to cross Hoving's threshold – over a decade earlier Hoving had successfully seen off a raid by Bulova, the prestige watch company. Thus, although he greeted Peter with perfect old world courtesy, Hoving wasted no time in delivering his trademark message to unsought callers with dubious intentions: "I have no need to sell and I will never, ever, do so."

Peter's reply was characteristic and was also to become standard. He explained politely his reasons for buying Tiffany stock and even more politely that Hoving's intentions were of marginal consequence to him. He was quite content to be patient and await the inevitable recognition of the fact that Tiffany shares were fundamentally undervalued. Hoving immediately thawed and in due course they became good friends.

Peter's assessment turned out to be entirely accurate and within a year he was able to sell his entire position at $19.00 and rub his hands contentedly. But six months later there was a "sting" when Avon Products made an all share offer for Tiffany worth $50.00 per share and Hoving unhesitatingly accepted it. Peter's comment was that he ought to have asked Hoving, "Never, ever – at any price?" This outcome prompted considerable discussion among the Cundill Value Fund board members over the question of how to deal with the problem of when to sell. Peter himself could come up with no absolutely satisfactory proposal for a formula. In the end the solution turned out to be something of a compromise: the fund would automatically sell half of any given position when it had doubled, in effect thereby writing down the cost of the remainder to zero with the fund manager then left with full discretion as to when to sell the balance. Peter expressed his collected thoughts in the journal, based on the first five years of his accumulated experience as a value investor.

> The ultimate skill in this business is in knowing when to make the judgement call to let profits run. While it is true that 99% of investment effort is routine, unspectacular enquiry, checking and double checking, laboriously building up a web of information with single threads until it constitutes a complete tableau, just occasionally a flash of inspiration may be necessary. Once we have begun to build a position it has to be recognized that our intentions may change in the course of its construction. An influential, or even controlling, position quite often results from a situation where a cheap security does little or nothing pricewise for such a long time that we are able to buy a significant percentage of the equity. Whether our intentions remain passive under these circumstances depends on an assessment of the outlook for the company and the capability of its management, but I don't think that we ought to be pro-active merely for the sake of it. My task is principally the identification of opportunity and the decision to press the buy button. This may sometimes turn out to be a catalyst in itself, but normally we should rely on others to do the promotional work or to put the company directly into play. Otherwise it will turn into a constant and time-consuming distraction from our prime objective of finding cheap securities to buy.

The perfect illustration of this axiom turned out to be right at the heart of Wall Street. In 1978, at prices of around \$6.00 a share, Peter had started to accumulate a position in Bache, a large and venerable brokerage house founded back in the 1870s. Bache had a book value of \$15.50 and Peter had calculated that, in a liquidation, if the bond portfolio were wound up and the debt paid off, the stock would be worth \$9.00, and this was without attributing any value to the fixed assets.

Bache's boss, Harry Jacobs, had recently fought off a run taken at his company by Gerry Tsai, a successful New York fund manager to whom Jacobs had declared, even more roundly than Walter Hoving had done when he met Peter, "I'm going to fight you to the death." And he had done so, buying Tsai's position at a premium to the market price, a practice known as "greenmailing," which today would attract the immediate attention of the SEC. Although it was not then illegal, Jacob's defence tactic had seriously annoyed his shareholders, who considered it highhanded and out of touch with the prevailing standards of good corporate practice. The operation had consequently left Bache in a position that was considerably more vulnerable to a predator.

Peter's reputation was now such that his investment activity was being carefully monitored by an increasing number of professional investors, especially on the buy side. This was particularly the case in Vancouver and so it came as no surprise to him to learn that First City Financial, Sam Belzberg's family holding company, was a significant buyer of Bache stock. Peter already knew Sam personally and Sam was a close associate of Maurice Strong, with whom he had co-invested in American Water Development Inc. The news did, however, come as a nasty surprise to Harry Jacobs, who considered the Belzbergs to be even less suitable purchasers than Jerry Tsai and, as First City filed its 13D, declaring a 5% interest, and then went on steadily buying, Jacobs panicked again.

His reaction was to cast around somewhat desperately for another investor whom he could persuade into taking a substantial position in Bache to fend off the Belzbergs. Eventually he came up with the Hunt brothers, Nelson and Bunker, who were just then beginning their famously ruinous foray into the silver market. Jacobs felt that he had pulled off a real coup – not only had he, as he supposed, checkmated the Belzbergs with the blue-blooded Hunts, but he had at the same time secured a huge client for Bache. The Hunts then began to try to corner the silver market, using Bache as their principal broker, and ran the price up from under $10 per ounce to over $50, all of it financed on margin, $250 million of it provided by Bache, an enormous sum at the time.

However, on 20 January 1980, the whole card-castle was brought crashing down by the Commodity Exchange which, prompted by the Federal Reserve's disapproval of the Hunt brothers' attempt to distort the normal conduct of commercial trading, suspended all new purchase orders in silver futures. The price of silver immediately collapsed and it then transpired that Bache had neglected to do its due diligence properly as to the Hunts' creditworthiness. They proved unable to meet their margin calls and Bache was forced to start dumping the silver positions it held on the Hunts' behalf, further aggravating the price decline.

Jacobs' defence strategy against the Belzbergs was now in tatters and, to add insult to injury, in their desperation the Hunts sold their own Bache stock directly to First City Financial, bringing the Belzberg holding up to 14%. The beleaguered Jacobs resorted to hiring private investigators to try to dig up some dirt on the Belzberg family and spread totally unfounded rumours that they had uncovered some disreputable mafia connections. Not surprisingly, Sam Belzberg was incensed, but, rather than responding with a law suit, he just carried on buying Bache stock even more aggressively, bringing his position up to 21%. By this time Jacobs was not only in mortal fear of losing control of his company but there was an acute risk of its actually going under as a result of the Hunts' inability to meet the full extent of their liabilities.

Two months later Peter was just sitting down to lunch in Vancouver with Sam Belzberg himself when they heard that Bache's shares had been suspended by the SEC and the company had announced that it was selling a further $200 million of silver belonging to Bunker Hunt. It was an extremely tense lunch. If Bache had actually gone bust the effect on both First City and the Cundill Value Fund would have been more than a little uncomfortable. Peter, however, remained confident that if it came to liquidation, even after the Hunt losses that Bache had incurred, he would still recover his cost, although there would be little or no profit and the fund would consequently take an unwelcome hit that might even undo his previously unblemished performance record.

Fortunately, bankrupting a major Wall Street firm with thousands of employees and tens of thousands of retail clients was not part of the Federal Reserve's plan and a few weeks later Bache sold out to the mighty Prudential Assurance, thereby bailing out the Belzbergs with a handsome profit of $40 million and Peter with an even bigger percentage gain. Although the calculated margin of safety had not actually been put to the test, its practical necessity had been underlined for Peter. Had he not been fully convinced that his work on Bache had established it beyond doubt, the interim period before Prudential's intervention would have put him through far more than a few restless nights and several fevered checks of his numbers.

The Bache investment success added substantial additional support to Peter's confidence in the value approach, and this was bolstered further when Sam Belzberg asked Peter to join him as his partner in First City Financial. In his customary methodical way he reviewed the pros and cons in the journal:

> Sam can be an abrasive character so I can see the value for him in having an "alter ego" with a calmer more measured style. He is certainly one of the best financial minds in the business and I would be happy working with him on a professional level. As far as I know he has never screwed anyone or been screwed and Meighen thinks highly of him. He has one of the most important attributes of the master investor because he is supremely capable of running counter to the herd. He seems to possess the ability to consider a situation in isolation, cutting himself off from the mill of general opinion. And he has the emotional confidence to remain calm when events appear to be indicating that he's wrong. However, there is a danger that we might not turn out to be compatible from a personality point of view and that would leave me high and dry, having given up all that I have achieved so far with the Value Fund. Nevertheless it is a flattering offer.

Peter had been fortunate in launching the newly focused Value Fund at a moment when there was a plethora of opportunities, especially in the US, and by the end of 1979 he had committed nearly 70% of the fund's assets to American company shares because they were statistically cheaper than those in the Canadian or other markets and the quality of corporate information was reliable and readily to hand. Concentrating the assets of the fund into a single securities market where there was an abundance of undervalued securities was never to be an issue that gave Peter pause. He was equally prepared to focus his buying power into relatively few stocks of whose merits he was absolutely convinced, rather than seeking the more conventional comfort zone of wide diversification. The US portfolio at this time comprised just twenty companies with the average fully constructed position representing between 3% and 6% of total assets. The results spoke for themselves – at the close of the Cundill Value Fund's fifth year of operations it was one of only eight Canadian and thirty-two American funds with a compound growth rate in excess of 30% in a universe of nearly eight hundred funds.

5

Going Global

IN SPITE OF PETER'S WILLINGNESS to concentrate a substantial percentage of the Value Fund's resources into a single market in which, at any given juncture, there might be a plentiful choice of value opportunities, he had taken the view early on that he would be prepared "to put money into anything, anywhere, provided that the downside is measurable and acceptable and the chances of a good profit appear to be better than 50%. I will not take gambles, but it is part of my job description to be ready to take very carefully calculated risks." One such risk was looking at securities and markets outside North America, a policy which he realized might be severely criticized if his investments did not work out according to plan.

As early as 1964 Peter had noted in the journal that Sweden, in spite of having a tiny population, was an exemplary technocracy, as a result of which it punched well above its weight in the industrial pecking order. The Volvo success story, though intriguing in itself, was fairly well known internationally, but Peter suspected that Volvo was not alone and that it might be worth his while to take a closer look at Sweden to see if its securities markets might reveal any hidden gems for the value buyer. Peter also felt that Sweden had some distinct advantages as a first tentative step outside North American markets:

it was small enough and sufficiently close knit that the economy ought to be relatively easy to understand and company annual reports were in English with clear, concise, and transparent presentations and accounting policies that followed American standards.

Before making up his mind to undertake the research, Peter spoke to Volvo's vice-president in New York, an important man in the company since the US was by far Volvo's biggest overseas market. He was sufficiently impressed by what the man had to say to ask him to organize a visit to the Volvo plant in Gothenberg and so, in late November 1977, Peter arrived in Stockholm for the first time, did his customary exploratory run round the city, and called on the securities analysts at the Bank International. He spent the following day at Volvo meeting the senior sales executives and their finance people, then toured the entire manufacturing plant, and finally test drove Volvo's new 343 model.

Back in Stockholm he visited the Stock Exchange and called on the Swedish Shareholders' Association, which he joined on the spot. He had lunch with the institutional sales team for Swedish securities at the Enskilda Bank, whom he described as "serious, bright and knowledgeable, but thoroughly demoralized by the world's total indifference to their market and its individual securities, no matter how cheap." He had dinner with Jahrle Kahre, one of the Enskilda fund managers, and took an immediate liking to him, finding plenty of common ground in their investment thinking as well as the all-important ingredient of a sense of humour. When Peter described his visit to the Swedish Shareholders' Association, Kahre laughed and commented that Swedes were like lemmings, addicted to associations, "if there were an association for three-legged pigs they would join it." Notwithstanding the Swedes' depressed attitude toward their domestic stock market, a month later Peter had done enough work to satisfy himself that Volvo was a genuine net-net opportunity and he began a buying program.

From this moment on, neglected, obscure, and misunderstood overseas markets were increasingly to become a much-exploited investment speciality of Peter's, yielding rich rewards over the years and adding an invaluable dimension to the fund that often significantly enhanced its performance, especially in periods when there was a scarcity of value opportunity in North America. There was nothing "ad hoc" about the way in which Peter addressed the process of international value investment. In every instance it had to be firmly based on a clear understanding of local accounting practices and how those might differ from accepted standards in North America. The fact that it was different, less transparent, or deliberately opaque was never a reason for ignoring or excluding a market or a security. Peter's attitude was "vive la difference"; if a balance sheet was hard to penetrate it was not just a challenge but an opportunity because the difficulties actually represented a "barrier to entry" even for the experienced professional investor and undoubtedly excluded all but the most sophisticated private investors.

The other aspect, which Peter considered to be a vital component of a successful international strategy, was building carefully constructed networks of locally based professionals who had a thorough understanding of value investment principles and would instinctively recognize a security that would potentially fit the Cundill Value Fund's investment criteria. Creating a network like this involved dozens and dozens of calls, many of them largely unproductive; finding kindred spirits was rather like panning for gold, but the precious commodity gradually appeared over the years and became a very powerful adjunct to the pure numerical research.

The process of "going global" was not in any sense a departure from Graham and Dodd principles. In reality it was the first example, not so much of "changing a winning game" as of adapting the framework to give it greater flexibility and enhance its effectiveness.

A year later, partly with advice from the research team at the Enskilda Bank, who were already part of the network, the Swedish portfolio was expanded to include a sizeable position in Volvo's original parent, SKF, and in due course both shares more than doubled. It took two years for the two investments to demonstrate their worth, but once the initial analytical work had been done, patience was all that was required; there were no special dramas to prompt any queasy moments of doubt since neither the earnings nor the dividend streams ever faltered. In 1999, nearly twenty years after Peter himself had sold out, Volvo was bought by Ford at over ten times the 1977 price, but it had long since ceased to qualify as a net-net.

After this first successful venture, monitoring overseas markets in the search for undiscovered gold-bearing lodes became a routine research procedure for the Value Fund. As Peter's confidence grew and his information network became more broadly international, he was increasingly prepared to reposition the Value Fund aggressively by shifting a significant percentage of its assets into one or more overseas markets, so that it would be fair to say that the policy he established, which still applies today, was never to favour domestic North American markets for their own sake but to be prepared to search exhaustively for global value, no matter where it might be tucked away. Over the years an international approach to value investment has become the hallmark of what is now, more than thirty years on, the Mackenzie Cundill group of funds.

The first few years of Peter's management of the Cundill Value Fund had been an unequivocal success and his confidence in the theoretical grounding of his investment approach, as well as its practical application and execution, had grown immeasurably in the process. It had not been without some uncomfortable moments and some unwelcome surprises, but in the final analysis the all-important margin of safety had always held good.

6

Swapping Continents

PETER'S WIFE, JOANIE, WAS USUALLY quite prepared to go along with him in some of the unusual ways in which he chose to live his life. She preferred North American habits and culture and was perfectly content being in British Columbia, Washington, or California, either by the coast or in the mountains, but by the mid 1980s Peter was becoming restless in Vancouver, especially as his professional life had begun to take on a considerably more international dimension. He was hankering after the chance to explore the possibility of taking up permanent residence outside Canada and the obvious choices were New York, Paris, or London.

He sensed that if he were to present Joanie with New York as an option straight away, the chance of ever persuading her to accept Europe would be lost. So he dangled the carrot of a three-month trial of what it would be like to live in Paris. He got his way and at the beginning of 1983 they arrived at Charles de Gaulle airport together to take possession of an apartment near the Étoile at the top of the Champs Élysées.

Peter was enthralled by the whole idea and was itching to get work on his French, armed with his old notebooks from French lessons in the 1960s. Joanie was nervous and uncomfortable:

So the great Parisian adventure begins. Our new apartment at 42 Rue Beaujon is charming, if a little sparse, and things may take time to understand, but we are in the heart of Paris. We spent the day doing the small things like shopping at Prisunic and it was hard for Joanie, so unfamiliar, even alien, and she had hysterics about losing a diamond earring – it was a bad day for her and we had a restless night on that account, but I'm enjoying the learning curve. Just the one-day "blues," however; an attractive looking guy from France Acceuil arrived to fix the lights and we had great technical discussions about "prises, vises, and aiguilles" and he smiled incessantly at Joanie in a uniquely Gallic manner. The French do tend to get very excited, rushing around trying out everything at least twice.

We went to a bistro in the Avenue Georges V for lunch – a hot dog – surrounded by beautiful quadroon models – must go again!

By the following evening Joanie had acclimatized herself and was beginning to enjoy the experience. Peter had taken her to the Pompidou Centre to see the Yves Klein exhibition during the day and that night they had dined at the Michelin three-star Tour d'Argent at a special table from which they could enjoy the romantic panorama of the Seine and the floodlit cathedral of Notre Dame while they ate their way through the restaurant's famous duckling. They went on to the Crazy Horse Saloon to see the world's most sophisticated strip show and then danced and caroused at the nearby Calvados bar until five in the morning, by which time Joanie was a convert.

From a professional point of view Peter was well-organized, with his own office at Bear Stearns, just a walk down the Champs Élysées from the apartment, an arrangement that suited him perfectly and which he did his best to replicate with a variety of different investment firms on all his later extended visits around the world. However, in the end it was Joanie, not Peter, who became truly enamoured of the idea of living in Paris. As he summed up his feelings about the experience:

> Somehow I feel I've wasted my time here. I didn't really learn much and actually got less joy out of life than I had expected. I suppose that I've developed a better understanding of France and things French and the language has improved considerably. I have matured some commercial ideas – more notably in Holland and Belgium than France. It hasn't helped that we have only had one day in the whole three months where it didn't rain at all. I'm more ready than usual for a vacation with sun and sea.

The real problem, however, was not that Paris was uncongenial, it was that Peter had very quickly realized that it was a financial backwater by comparison with London so that, from a professional standpoint, he might just as well be in Vancouver. London was beckoning and he was not at all certain how that alternative would play with Joanie, who was so freshly converted to Parisian life. As he confessed to himself after a leisurely Sunday breakfast at Claridges:

> Bacon, eggs, sausages, toast and marmalade, and all the Sunday papers – I love the UK. It's a man's world. But J, despite her limited French has, I fear, fallen for Paris. It's not going to be easy to move over here.

But by the time Peter returned to Canada his mind had been made up – he was moving to Europe and it was definitely going to be to London. But prior to anything else there was another marathon to be run and he was determined that this one was to be the elusive sub-3.

It was 1983 and the year was already filled with anniversaries: ten years of marriage, twenty years of writing the journal, and ten years since the acquisition of the All Canadian Venture Fund, which had become the Cundill Value Fund. It was the perfect moment to aim for it. Training immediately began in earnest and Peter worked steadily on his speed and stamina through to the end of September, when he did his final pre-race run:

> Ran my last 20 miles almost as a farewell tour of Montreal, up Sherbrooke, through Montreal West – Cote Saint Luc – Cavendish Boulevard, around the school grounds of Lower Canada College as Ashbury were playing LCC – but no crowd and no headmaster – then back along Westmount Boulevard and Côte des Neiges, I stopped at the Hillside for a coke and lastly back along Saint Catherine's to the Ritz. It was very nostalgic and I ran by my old apartment. I had dinner with old friends at Papineau, lovely food, followed by a champagne reunion at the 4 Seasons and in bed by 2. All in all a great conceptual good-bye. I'm now beginning to think of myself as a 'non-res'.

A week later in Portland, Oregon, Peter woke at 5 am, treated himself to a juice, a cup of coffee, and a banana, and took a cab to the Coliseum where he joined 2,400 other starters on a cool, overcast morning. The race was downhill at the start and, with the temperature at 54 degrees, the conditions were ideal. The field got a spritzer of rain at the perfect moment at about mile twenty and Peter ran a consistently strong race, speeding up at intervals and then settling back to a steady, sustainable pace. His technique had improved; he had learned to allow his knees to drop down and come back up steadily and the confidence he had built up in his own fitness gave him the added strength to overcome "the wall." He actually ran miles twenty to twenty-five in just thirty-four minutes, almost sprinting from miles twenty-one to twenty-two, pacing with a runner coming up behind him and staying with him to achieve the six minute mile which ensured that he made the finishing line in 2:59. He was ecstatic and after several baths and Jacuzzis the champagne flowed until 10:30, when he finally faded.

In the meantime Peter had successfully negotiated a "trial" residence in London with Joanie and they had arrived together at Heathrow in the spring of 1984 feeling like immigrants, with Peter wearing his smartest suit, complete with waistcoat, in order to impress the officials at passport control. Of course, there was no difficulty at all and they moved into an apartment on Walton Street, not far from Harrods. After a few days he described his impressions:

> London to live in will, I rather imagine, be a mixture of the drab and the graceful. At dusk the city is superb; full of mysterious allure and with its blemishes softened. The huge choice of parks is a source of endless pleasure – like nowhere else. It is a paradise for a runner. The tube, however, is ghastly – normal food pretty awful, not a patch on New York or Paris, although Mark's Club is excellent.

7

A Decade of Success

IN 1984 THE CUNDILL VALUE FUND celebrated its tenth year of operation under Peter's management. The result for the year was an appreciation of 6%, which might have been considered disappointing by contrast with the 44% gain it had enjoyed the previous year, but, since this compared with a 4% decline in the Dow Jones and a 6% decline in the Toronto Stock Exchange, Peter still had reason to be well pleased. The fund had virtually doubled in size over the year to $126 million, so that it could no longer be considered just a small "hot shot" affair, relying for its performance on an ability to invest in the type of small, illiquid, contrarian securities that were out of the question for bigger funds. Peter took the opportunity to review the fund's success in the Annual Report for that year:

> We have now completed 10 years using the Graham and Dodd approach to investment. This period has witnessed a compound return on shareholder's equity of 26% per annum.
>
> We have learned much during the past 10 years:
>
> - The value method of investing will tend at least to give compound rates of return in the high teens over longer periods of time.

- There will be losing years; but if the art of making money is not to lose it, then there should not be substantial losses.
- The fund will tend to do better in slightly down to indifferent markets and not to do as well as our growth-orientated colleagues in good markets.
- It is ever more challenging to perform well with a larger fund. With increased size the diversification means that no individual investment, whether a gain or a loss, will have a dramatic effect on the unit price.
- We have developed a global approach to investing. As a result, we have a far broader range of securities to choose from than any purely domestic or North American fund.
- We have developed a network of contacts around the world who are like-minded in value orientation.
- We have gradually modified our approach from a straight formula valuation basis to one where we try to buy securities selling below liquidation value, taking into consideration off-balance sheet items.
- THE MOST IMPORTANT ATTRIBUTE FOR SUCCESS IN VALUE INVESTING IS PATIENCE, PATIENCE, AND MORE PATIENCE. THE MAJORITY OF INVESTORS DO NOT POSSESS THIS CHARACTERISTIC.

As a result of the success of this methodology, more interest in this kind of investing has developed and newcomers have been attracted to the field. Notwithstanding this, as Warren Buffett recently wrote "the secret has been out for fifty years, ever since Graham and Dodd wrote *Security Analysis*. So far there has been no discernable erosion in the wide discrepancies between price and value in the marketplace."

The journals at this time also contain a cluster of nuggets from Peter's investment thinking, combined with the occasional quotation that had struck him as relevant:

> I don't much believe in institutions and I certainly don't believe in mere formulae. The authority of both can be pernicious and destructive. It is worth remembering that many of the world's most renowned organizations are fundamentally flawed as well as irrational – the Jesuits, the Mafia, and IBM. As far as generally available analysis is concerned, often what sounds terrible is just the truth and what sounds great is nothing but fantasy and rubbish. There should never be commitments "in principle," only bargains based on verifiable fact. It is also dangerous to rely on a single strategy in a doctrinaire fashion. Strategies and disciplines ought always to be tempered by intelligence and intuition.
>
> It is vital not to confuse a global approach to investing with having a global view. I am suspicious of global views. The world as I see it is still deeply entrenched in its regional peculiarities and in many ways it is just these peculiarities that offer opportunity to the global value scavenger. St. Matthew put it even better "Where so ever the carcass is, there will the eagles be gathered together."
>
> For all my emphasis on the virtues of patience in value investment it has to go hand in hand with minute attention to the detail, with conviction and determination, otherwise patience is just futile endurance.

> Oscar Wilde said that "consistency" is the last refuge of the unimaginative, but this is not the same as "routines." I believe that routines can actually be a support, rendering the imaginative process more effective in action – preventing the kind of superfluity of ideas that promotes dithering and constipates action.

Peter's global approach to value investment had taken distinct shape over the Value Fund's first decade. Through his travelling and his growing reputation he had succeeded in building up an enviable network of contacts who understood his investment concept; from John Templeton in Nassau, who had invested $5 million in the fund, and Nathaniel de Rothschild in Paris, to Michael Milken and Peter Ackerman at Drexel Burnham in Los Angeles, as well as Irving Kahn and Mike Price in New York, Niels Taub and Jim Slater in London, Don Kennedy in San Francisco, and Chris Ondaatje and Sam Belzberg in Canada, and this is far from an exhaustive list. Beyond these there were good connections with the Jardine Fleming people in Hong Kong, with the Enskilda Bank in Sweden, DeWaay in Brussels, Pierson, Heldring & Pierson in Amsterdam, Nomura in Tokyo, Warburg in London, Deutsche Bank, and Paribas.

In addition Peter had become acquainted with many others who already were, or were to become, significant operators in the corporate world, such as Peter Munk, Edgar Kaiser, Conrad Black, Monty Gordon, Peter Brown, and Asher Edelman, to name but a few. Not only were such associates a useful sounding board for investment ideas but, in a sense, some of them served as role models or, perhaps more accurately in the post-Trebell era, as rulers against which Peter could measure himself, as he did in the case of Asher Edelman:

> Asher just keeps on driving – energy, attention to detail, and a

real sense of balance in his life. But I believe it is his ambition that is the power-house. Am I just settling into a comfortable pew? When I had dinner at Asher's house we had chicken and champagne all perfectly served and all the guests were so disciplined, just tasting and sipping. They maintain that having a hangover is a waste of a day. I agree, but it's fun getting there and I wanted to party – maybe it's a skill I need to acquire, Asher's three-year record is actually better than mine.

And Sam Belzberg;

Sam has a love of negotiation and especially for the "underside" of a deal; he has a knack of getting to the heart of the matter and he is very hard to read. These are all skills that I want to develop. He has a pirate's instincts, a capacity to spot the opposition's Achilles heel; he once quoted me an Inuit saying, "The wolf keeps the caribou strong."

The Cundill Conference had by now become a fixed annual event; a forum at which Peter's friends, colleagues, and business associates could meet once a year in a stimulating environment that was both private and quite informal. The format was well conceived. The opening morning was invariably an investment discussion devoted to a specific topic, such as Chapter XI corporate bankruptcy for example, and although each session was led by an expert, it was always open to the floor, which had the effect of promoting lively discussion amongst a gathering of some of the best professional minds in the business.

External speakers of very high quality were engaged to address the conference lunches on subjects that bore no direct relation to the world of finance. Notwithstanding, they were popular and well attended, with very few people being tempted to "slope off" in private gaggles, and the speakers often succeeded in stimulating Peter's own thinking along useful lateral paths:

> We are attached to a star of only average size, in a galaxy of only average size and very far from the heart of the action where new stars are being born all the time and new galaxies are forming. A single galaxy can contain a billion stars and there are probably more than a billion galaxies. It's a tough perspective to grasp, but a good antidote to hubris.

> My attitude to research is like the Korean potters we heard about. Their clay has to make itself manifest – one subtle shade is gradually superimposed on another until the whole pot is pulsating with translucent colour. Research also has to work out its destiny. The point is to achieve a profound perception, not necessarily a wide perspective.

> Maybe the ice cap is melting at the moment but there will doubtless be other ice ages. Predicting seismic or cosmological changes in the earth's life cycle is probably even less accurate than trying to anticipate the fluctuations of the market and, for the purpose of determining action, just as useless. The challenge of trying to comprehend the universe is another matter.

The food and the wine at the conferences was always first class and there was usually a trip to the theatre followed by a dinner at one of the top restaurants in the host city. The second morning soon came to be known as "Pete's Morning," where he would take the floor at about 9:00 am in shirtsleeves, wearing a short-sleeved pale blue cashmere sweater, and proceed, in his own inimitable, rambling style, to hold the audience's attention for a full three hours with investment stories, case studies, and his particular brand of distilled wisdom. From time to time he would call on someone from the floor to elaborate on his theme or support an argument with further expert knowledge.

After lunch the conference broke up until the cocktail hour and this was followed by the closing dinner, at which there were no speeches and Peter himself would address his first dry martini in a week and declare party time, adjourning for some of the "wild dancing" for which he was also famed, accompanied by a massive Churchillian Havana cigar (smuggled if the venue were in the USA) and quantities of champagne and brandy. It is hardly surprising that a Cundill Conference invitation quickly became a very sought-after ticket.

Astonishingly, for an obscure western Canadian-based fund with a niche strategy, its first pension fund client turned out to be the Paris-based Caisse Centrale des Banques Populaires, which had elected to make the investment on behalf of its own pensioners. The second client was the Air France Pension Fund and it would be very surprising if any other domestically incorporated Canadian fund could ever have boasted such a clientele. By the end of 1985 overseas investment outside the United States accounted for 15% of the portfolio, with investments in the United Kingdom, Japan, Sweden, the Netherlands, and Australia. Peter's reputation as a global bargain hunter was well on the road and it was supported by his decision to move to London, which, then as now, was the most international of any of the major financial centres, with its geographical location straddling the time zones between North America and Asia.

8

New Dimensions

AS WORD OF PETER'S FINANCIAL wizardry spread through the wider community, he was frequently asked to undertake charity work, much of which he had to decline because he recognized that spreading his efforts too thinly was just a waste of everyone's time. However, he did accept Bryan Reynolds's suggestion that he should join the board of trustees of Pearson College. It was the second oldest school in the United World Colleges group, the first of which had been founded in Wales shortly after the Second World War under the auspices of Kurt Hahn, the great German educationalist and liberal thinker.

Hahn's ideas very much coincided with some of Peter's own thoughts about what ought to form the best principles for an effective modern education, especially the need to place equal emphasis on training both the mind and the body. UWC had always advocated an elitist approach based not on background, wealth, or social standing but on individual merit, and its overall ambition was to foster a supranational caucus of alumni with shared experiences and values, all of which fit perfectly with Peter's views.

He was deeply impressed by his first visit. The college is set in a beautiful campus on seventy-five acres at the edge of the Pacific Ocean at the southern tip of Vancouver Island, which provides the students with every possible outdoor sporting opportunity and spectacular surroundings that are home to deer, eagles, otters, seals, and whales. Peter spent the day in distinguished company: Prince Charles was there in his capacity as patron and at his best, chatting with the trustees and the students, accompanied by Lord Mountbatten's grandson Lord Romsey. Peter was flattered to be asked to assume the chairmanship of the College Investment Committee, which he willingly accepted, immediately reciprocating the compliment with a generous contribution towards funding the new library. But, however glamorous the role might appear to be, Peter always retained a lively appreciation of the underlying functionality of "charity" work:

> The boards of charitable foundations are convenient meeting places for influential people. Their ostensible purpose is intimately bound up with the social and commercial ones.

The "Adviser Profile" in the 1984 Annual report describes London as:

> the central listening post from which Peter Cundill monitors market activities in the Far East, the United States, Europe, Canada, and the rest of the world. He has an entrepreneurial spirit and the discipline of an athlete who, in middle age, can still run a marathon in under three hours. He does not act on tips. He combs the stock exchanges of the world and pores over the annual reports, makes his own calculations and visits the corporate locations himself, always asking the underlying question, "Would I personally want to buy this business? And if so, how much would I be prepared to pay for it, in full knowledge of its true net worth?" The entire process is summed up in the

slogan that was now adopted for the Value Fund: 'Buying a Dollar for Forty Cents.'

Peter was very keen that the members of the Value Fund board should thoroughly understand the business rationale behind his decision to relocate. With this in mind he decided to hold a board meeting in London so that they could see for themselves. The meeting was held at the Savoy Hotel, close to the City, and it was followed by a cocktail party for about a hundred people, attended by a good sprinkling of senior members of the banking, investment, and brokerage fraternities as well as the Canadian community in London. The board were suitably impressed and, if they had been harbouring any doubts about the wisdom of the move from the perspective of the fund, these were permanently shelved.

There was a further dimension to London as a location in those days that made it reasonable for the city to lay claim to being the most conveniently placed international community in the world. It was the era of the supersonic Concorde, which had begun its thirty-year flying career in 1969, making it possible to travel from London to New York in a mere three and a half hours. By the middle of the 1980s it had attained the status of a commuter flight for those for whom time was money. In fact it had become possible to take the 10 am Concorde flight from London, arrive in New York at 8:30 am local time, take the helicopter service into Manhattan for a meeting at 9:30 am, and then return to London after an early working lunch, arriving back at Heathrow at 10 pm and ending up in central London an hour later – a long day, but not extraordinarily so. It did not, of course, work quite so well in reverse for residents of New York, which simply added to the attraction of London. Peter quickly became a regular Concorde passenger and commented:

The Concorde is a sort of club in the air for the world's top 10,000. I never fail to meet friends and business associates in the departure lounge, or seated beside me on the flight, and there is something about flying in the stratosphere at twice the speed of sound which seems to inspire the exchange of confidences. It is a remarkable sounding board, especially in my world of matters financial. For me some of these conversations are invaluable from the point of view of insights and perspectives. One becomes even more keenly aware that there is never just one factor determining events, there are many of them interwoven and acting simultaneously. Indeed, from my own professional standpoint, I always need to discipline myself to be aware of the world generally, rather than trying to be specific. I only need to be specific about the numbers. Funnily enough, having travelled on the Air France Concorde flight from Paris into Washington, I found it was not at all the same experience, at least not for those in my line of business, perhaps it may be for diplomats, politicians, and bureaucrats.

Of course not all of Peter's travelling could be accomplished on the Concorde and his increasing focus on Japan meant that he was ever keener to establish a network of individuals who had a thorough understanding of value investment, not just in London and Hong Kong but in Tokyo itself, and he was equally determined to get really "under the skin" of Japanese corporate structures and culture. With this in mind he made his second trip to Japan towards the end of August 1985 and he described it in some detail:

To Tokyo via Anchorage. The transit lounge was my "welcome" to Japan – hundreds of bustling Japanese tourists being shepherded along by American staff, desperate to get to the shopping and buy up all the famous European fashion labels; not something I had witnessed before. This is the meeting point between East and West!

I had forgotten how far it is from Narita Airport into Tokyo: 40 miles. My strongest impression was of the sun, which I never saw in March 1969 – 85 degrees of heat and 95% humidity. I checked in and then swam and sat outside watching the leanest whippet of a man practising his karate moves. All the bodies around are very low fat, fitness appears to be in vogue as well as western fashions. The subway was a lonely experience without a guide. I just encountered blank stares, but managed to work it out by myself in the end, but it emphasized the reality that Japan is still deeply insular. The taste for anything international is very superficial, just a veneer.

On this visit the round of meetings was carefully oriented towards discovering whether there were any people in the Tokyo financial community who were familiar with Graham and Dodd principles, especially if they were Japanese. Both Sumitomo Trust and Nomura yielded individuals who spoke the value language and interacted well with Peter and he also managed to find an executive at Nikko Securities, Kaneko-san, who was familiar with both Benjamin Graham's *Security Analysis* and *The Intelligent Investor.*

They had an excellent discussion from which Peter gleaned that his hunch was correct and that there was a considerable choice of Japanese securities trading at below book value and probably below liquidation value, particularly in the banking and insurance sectors, where many of the companies owned significant portfolios of securities that were carried at cost on the balance sheet, rather than at market value. Peter went on to visit the Tokyo Stock Exchange in a mood of excited anticipation and then spent the afternoon in the Tokyo Metropolitan Museum where he could look and think at the same time:

> It was formerly a nobleman's house, built in the "art deco" style. There was an exhibition of Indian painting which didn't appear to be attracting much attention, but the grounds were truly peaceful and solitude is something to be treasured here. There is a quality of stillness at the core of the Japanese psyche which lends the people real strength and fortitude. This evening the heat and humidity were not quite so oppressive as I walked in the streets smoking a cigar.
>
> My overall impression is that over the next 20 years the Japanese will be the world's dominant economic force. Alliances will form around them and conversely against them. I have always assumed that the Anglo-Saxon races were the most civilized, best organized, and brightest as well as being fine warriors. We are not; by comparison with the Japanese we are impolite, undisciplined, and uncivilized. Against this, North America's strengths are its natural resources, its flexibility, and its individual creative capacity.

By the end of 1985 Peter had begun cautiously to invest in Japan so that by the end of the following year Japanese securities represented just under 3% of the assets of the Value Fund.

9

Investments and Stratagems

THE LEADING POSITION that the Value Fund had assumed in North American performance tables had automatically drawn Peter into the "limelight," so that by the early 1980s the financial press was keenly aware of him, eager to interview him and to write about him, particularly as he was no dry back-room boffin but a frank and effective communicator with a wry sense of humour. In addition to which he was an athlete of some note and he led the kind of jet-set international lifestyle that, with the zest of a little eccentricity, suited the mood of the times.

As a result there were frequent articles about him and he was individually featured in volume two of Peter Newman's much acclaimed book, *The Acquisitors,* the first volume of which had been Canada's biggest ever best-seller, running into several editions and selling 300,000 copies. It had turned into far more than just an account of Canada's business community, being described by J.K. Galbraith as "the best guide anyone will ever encounter to Canada." It was a kind of "Who's Who," incorporating a blend of brilliantly told anecdote and serious social history. The second volume was to be equally successful, with its description of the new generation of Canada's business elite, who were rapidly becoming household names themselves. After reading the piece written about him, Peter wisely commented:

> If you are going to live in the public eye, you will have to accept what's said about you without taking it too seriously, whether good or bad.

In actual fact what Newman had to say was extremely laudatory, although the personal description might have been considered a little fanciful: "He has the feverish mien of an anthropology professor seeking tenure – all vulnerability, awkward limb movements, and beseeching eyes." But there were also some interesting secrets revealed, since Newman refers to Peter acting as a financial advisor to the McConnell estate though Starlaw Investments Ltd, to the Bronfman family through Cemp Investments, as well as the Woodwards and the Belzbergs. He goes on to discuss Peter's "solid and impressive" connections with the establishment of eastern Canada through his uncle, Peter Scott, who in the 1950s and 60s had helped to build Wood Gundy into Canada's premier investment bank. Political affiliations are also referred to, including Peter's participation on the advisory council of Joe Clark, the leader of the Tory party in Canada, and Newman remarked especially on the way in which Peter was deliberately constructing an international network to support his view that the value investment universe ought not to be subject to frontiers or boundaries, other than those of the value investment discipline itself.

Peter also appeared on the front cover of an issue of *Equity*, on which he commented:

> Read the "Equity" piece with my picture on the front. It is the lead story. If one reads it quickly, as would the average reader, it is very flattering. A more careful reading reveals a slightly

> different picture with which I have no real quarrel. You have to learn to take the bad along with the good.

Peter felt that the Equity piece did not give sufficient weight to his serious professionalism. However the independent assessment of Peter and his investment record was unequivocally favourable. The investment community was beginning to take notice, as is evidenced by a letter he received at the time from the head of Wood Gundy's asset management arm:

> We believe that numbers alone don't make history; people do! Just as important as outstanding numbers is the outstanding group of people who make such successes possible, over and over again.
>
> I had the pleasure yesterday of attending your annual meeting in Toronto and I enjoyed your presentation and its content; although your "looks" aren't nearly as attractive as your "numbers" [!?], it is always a pleasure to put a face and a personality to products.
>
> With a real desire to get to know you and your organization a little better, I would ask that you consider a short visit to us at a convenient time on one of your trips to Toronto.

Where this may have led is not recorded, but Peter kept the letter.

The 1980s were filled with compelling investment stories out of the Cundill Value Fund stable of discoveries and there were some all-time classics, one of which was Cleveland Cliffs. The company was in a sense the equivalent of a producer of "widgets"; it was North America's largest supplier of iron ore pellets, an old style "muck and brass" kind of operation that was of little interest in an investment world that was becoming obsessed with technology and companies with "unlimited" growth potential. Cliffs surfaced on the radar screen through Alan Kahn, an increasingly influential member of Peter's network. It was a potential net-net, although not a pure one because it was a participant in a series of joint ventures that could not strictly be regarded as liquid assets, however solid they might be. Nevertheless, it was a neglected security. The shares had fallen from just under $40 in mid 1980 to $18 at the beginning of 1985; book value had also declined over the same period, but from $30 to $22. As Peter examined Cliffs more closely, he noticed that the company owned a power plant in Michigan that was carried on the balance sheet at a negligible value and he began to wonder whether this might not be an additional and hidden asset, the golden nugget that would constitute the margin of safety, perhaps even the catalyst for public recognition.

By the second half of the 1980s Peter was in the habit of calling on the group of like-minded "net-netter's" that he had so carefully cultivated to back up his research independently. He was aware Alan Kahn had already done some work on power plants in Arizona and he called him in great excitement to ask him to have a look at Cliffs' Michigan facility. About ten days later Peter received an equally excited return call from the visit. Alan was virtually incoherent with enthusiasm, the plant was, he said, "worth a zillion dollars." Peter's eyebrows went up a fraction at this, but he wasted no time in calling for a second opinion from Don Kennedy in San Francisco, another value player who had a good understanding of the power industry as well as a usefully sceptical approach to analysis.

Don's endorsement was more cautious but he had no hesitation in confirming that he was also convinced that the plant was worth "a lot of money" and so Peter started to buy Cliffs at $15.00 and the stock proceeded to slide relentlessly month after month. Peter,

Don Kennedy, and the Kahns appeared to be the only buyers in a market awash with institutional and retail sellers who simply wanted to be out of such a "dog of a security" at any price so that they could make use of the proceeds in the more promising area of computer software development.

Of the three buyers Peter was by far the largest, and it took a steady nerve and utter conviction, especially as another very large seller came out of the woodwork in the fall. It seemed that every time Peter bought a block of stock, another would promptly be offered. Years later he recalled standing on the steps of the Metropolitan Club in New York with Don Kennedy in that November, splitting up what had been their latest block purchase at $6.00 and wondering whether it might just turn out to be the "last hurrah." It was – the selling pressure began to ease after that. By then the fund owned well over 100,000 shares at an average price of $9.75, representing nearly 4 per cent of total assets.

By the spring of 1987 the long bull market was entering its final euphoric phase, carrying everything with it, even solid old companies like Cliffs, as investors finally began to scour the indices for asset values and take-over candidates. By July Cliffs had hit $20, triggering the Cundill rule that half the position should be sold when any holding had doubled. By the time of the October stock market crash Peter had unloaded about 15 per cent of the position at an average of around $19.00. Over the next few weeks the shares plummeted once again, and without hesitation Peter bought back all that he had sold, and more on top, at an average price of $10.

The fund then held the majority of the position until 1990 when most of it was sold and the last of it went in 1991. The compound rate of return was over 30 per cent. The margin of safety had served Peter well, but it had still required a steady nerve and plenty of patience and he later wrote:

> None of the great investments come easily. There is almost always a major blip for whatever reason and we have learnt to expect it and not to panic.

It had been possible to revisit Cliffs successfully because a major market crash had intervened after the company's underlying value had begun to be recognized by the wider investment community. Down-draughts of that kind tend to be regarded as "gifts from heaven" for disciples of Ben Graham and value investors tend to hold significant proportions of cash at most times, so that they are in a position to take advantage. Of course, no true value investor would claim to be able to predict the swings of the market and would never make any attempt to time either buying or selling on the basis of other people's market predictions.

However, the value discipline has an intrinsic tendency toward the accurate prediction of major trends. In purely practical terms, when the stock market is at or near a peak, there are likely to be very few, if any, bargains to be had and securities actually selling below liquidation value will be even scarcer. There is, therefore, a naturally induced bias towards selling and building cash during such periods, when investments within a value portfolio reach and surpass book value and continue upward to become statistically overvalued. This is not to suggest that it makes the selling judgement straightforward or easy for the value investor – in fact it probably militates towards selling too early and often towards buying too early as well. What it does do, however, is to considerably reduce the likely volatility of the portfolio and bolster the margin of safety, reinforcing the potency of the dictum that the secret of making money over the long term is not to lose it. It led Peter to a conclusion to which he frequently returns in his president's letters to the Cundill Value Fund shareholders:

> The "value method of investing" will tend to give better results in slightly down to indifferent markets and less relatively sparkling results in a raging bull market. What matters, however, is that the method will provide a consistent compound return in the middle teens over very long periods of time.

However, the more that Peter began to explore some of the by-ways of value, the more some slightly divergent avenues began to make investment sense. The first of these was the potential attraction of "holding companies," which he had started to notice very early in the life of the fund. More often than not holding companies are disliked by ordinary investors, both institutional and retail, as being difficult to understand, without the simplicity of a single clearly identifiable business, and sometimes requiring skilled "forensic" accountancy to arrive at any meaningful and reliable analysis.

For Peter, of course, such technical complication presented little difficulty and he soon discovered that holding companies, far from being minefields, quite often turned out to be treasure troves. They were simply an example of where his own well-honed professional accountancy skills could be utilized most effectively to exploit the advantages of the value methodology.

Anglo American Corp was the first real holding company in which Peter invested and it was drawn to his attention by Don Kennedy as early as 1976. It was the start of a long and happy association with Oppenheimer companies. Anglo has never been other than a very well run company, with extremely reliable reporting standards, but its exposure to diamonds, gold, and base metals made it subject both to investment fashion and cyclicality and those two factors have been responsible over several decades for a number of opportunities for the value buyer.

There is a note in Peter's research books about material he presented to the Value Fund board members, some of whom were inclined to be sceptical about whether the fund ought to be exposed to any markets that could be viewed as carrying a serious element of political risk. The note tells the company's story, gives a very clear picture of Anglo's appeal, and sells the concept of the investment with useful precision. It is a cogently argued case study that illustrates some of the nuances of Peter's own interpretation of how to work most effectively within the value framework without adhering slavishly to it. In later years most of the information would have been logged onto one of Peter's specially designed net-net sheets (see 225) which were to become the backbone of the Cundill process of investment analysis and still remain in regular use:

> Anglo American is a South African holding and management company providing a complete range of technical and administrative services to 285 companies worldwide. In addition they hold significant equity interests in a group of international mining, industrial, and investment companies including De Beers, Engelhard, Charter Consolidated, Hudson's Bay Mining and Smelting, Amax, and Anglo American Gold.
>
> De Beers controls over 80% of the world's diamond output and Anglo's investment has a market value of over $200 million. Anglo's mining interests last year produced 29% of the Free World's gold production and substantial quantities of coal, uranium, copper, iron ore, platinum, nickel, and zinc. They have invested in a number of successful petroleum consortia in the UK and Dutch sectors of the North Sea, including the Forties and Argyll fields. Through Charter Consolidated they have a sizeable interest in Rio Tinto Zinc. Anglo American of

Canada owns 38.5% of Hudson Bay Mining and Smelting. There are smaller, but still not insignificant, investments in timber, real estate, asbestos, potash, and citrus fruit groves.

Anglo is holding cash and equivalents of $235 million. Their investment portfolio is carried at a cost of $600 million against a value for the quoted securities alone of $1.1 billion. The shares at $2.50 are selling at a ten year low with a capitalization of a mere $313 million, the company is profitable (will earn about 60 cents this year), and the dividend yield is 10% and more than twice covered. The numbers are solid but the share price is clearly signalling a problem or problems – precisely what we like to see.

As I see it, first of all there is the gold price, which has recently sunk back from $170 and is now teetering on the brink of $100, and I take this to be a psychologically important resistance point which may or may not hold. At the same time mining costs have risen sharply, so it would be sensible to assume that Anglo's dividend stream from its gold-producing subsidiary will be substantially reduced for the next little while. In a worst case scenario this could lop about 20% off the earnings, but still leave the dividend twice covered – a considerable margin of safety in itself and the debt/equity ratio at 0.7 is more than satisfactory. As to the direction of the gold price – who can tell, but this is an unsettled and inflationary era and it is not hard to imagine a further rush of financial assets to safe havens, one of which is gold.

The other problem is clearly the politics, with the harbingers of doom predicting a collapse of order as black South Africans press more violently for equality, the demise of white supremacy, and a fair share of their birthright. The risks of labour unrest are undoubtedly real and might include sabotage and the spectre of expropriation if things really got out of hand. My instinct is that the worst case scenario is highly unlikely and, even if it were to happen, Anglo's internationally acknowledged expertise is in mine-management and someone would still have to manage the expropriated mines. However the true margin of safety lies in the diversified portfolio of assets outside South Africa.

Peter bought Anglo American for the fund in 1977 and sold it in 1979. The gain was over 100%.

Another avenue among the by-ways of value whose potential Peter quickly came to appreciate was distressed securities. His interest had originally been stirred through the work he had done on the liquidation of the Commonwealth Trust Company in BC in the early seventies, while he was at the Yorkshire Trust. The thing that had surprised him about this work was the sizeable and highly profitable realizations that the real estate portfolio had achieved as the liquidation process progressed and that, under the protective umbrella of the bankruptcy, these sales had taken place in an orderly fashion, not a fire-sale.

Then, shortly after he joined the board of the American Investment Corporation in 1979, Alan Johnson, AIC's legal counsel and a fellow director, had introduced Peter to Tony Novelly. Their first meeting was over a dinner, during which copious quantities of white wine were consumed, and the two formed an immediate bond. During dinner Novelly turned to Johnson and said:

"I like this guy Cundill, I want him on my board."
To which Johnson replied
"Tony, you don't have a board."
There was moment's silence before Novelly responded:
"Well you'd better get me one!"

It was the era of the Savings and Loan crises and real estate investment trusts (REITS) were falling by the wayside in large numbers, many of them destined either for liquidation or reorganization. Novelly had himself taken a position in Moraga Corporation, a California-based REIT that was in trouble, and Peter had recounted his own experience with Commonwealth Trust and had expressed an interest in the possibilities of investing in the distressed REIT market.

A day or two later he received a call, arranged by Novelly, from Geoff Newman at the Los Angeles office of Drexel Burnham Lambert offering him some bonds in another REIT that was actually in Chapter XI reorganization. Peter declined the offer but made arrangements to visit the Drexel office on his next trip to LA. When he turned up a month later he found a small but dynamic and extremely focused group. He was introduced to a young man named Michael Milken, who was brimming with energy and ideas, as well as to Peter Ackerman, who took the trouble to lead Peter into the complex world of distressed debt in spite of the relative insignificance of the funds that he then had under management.

Peter quickly forged a close relationship with the Drexel team, especially Peter Ackerman, who became a lifelong friend, and in the years prior to Drexel's fall from grace they became his principal brokers. The distressed debt element of the value fund portfolio at times amounted to as much as 20% of the total and contributed some stellar results.

The analytical process was in every respect in harmony with Grahamite principles, relying as it did primarily on balance sheet evaluation and hard liquidation values, accompanied by a detailed examination of the relevant indentures relating to the particular debenture issue. A thorough understanding of every nuance of the small print was vital to determining each issue's position in the pecking order of creditors and it was absolutely imperative to feel on firm ground about this should one ever be obliged to enter into negotiations about an eventual settlement or the terms of an issuer's emergence from bankruptcy.

In 1985 the Cundill Value Fund had returned a highly satisfactory 22%, but the early part of 1986 was proving to be rather problematic. Stock markets across the globe were extremely frothy, with the more speculative growth stocks leading the pack. Value securities were being left to languish and there was, in any case, a scarcity of value-based opportunities. By the early summer Peter was becoming frustrated as he set off for his annual hiking holiday in the Swiss Alps.

> I did some numbers while waiting for the flight to Lyons. We are making money in absolute terms, which is fine, but in relative terms it's awful. We manage $333 million of which 34% is in cash, but we have far too many holdings. I am tense because of the lack of performance, insecure and off form, which tends to make me aggressive and adopt a tone that jars.

As was often the case, Peter was taking a hyper-critical attitude to his performance. The Value Fund's record was outstanding and 1986 was simply proving to be an unavoidable hiatus. With a dearth of shares that qualified under strict value criteria, the temptation was always to lose patience and compromise, a temptation to which Peter very rarely succumbed. However, cash kept building up relentlessly in the fund as the markets rose to dizzier and dizzier heights and the holdings became statistically "overvalued" and, therefore, subject to automatic pruning. A lot of self-discipline was essential to avoid straying from the value framework and in Peter's case this was always accompanied by a good deal of soul-searching.

Peter's strictures about the proliferation of individual shares in the portfolio was one that consistently worried him because experience had convinced him that concentration was almost always an important factor in achieving superior performance. But in this instance the criticism was not entirely justified. The Value Fund's top ten holdings still represented 30% of assets and cash stood at a little over 30%. What had occurred was that a number of companies in which he had intended to build up a full position had run away in price before it had been possible to accumulate a normal-sized holding and there were quite a few other smallish holdings that had been introduced by way of having of an initial "look and see." However, resting on laurels was never part of the Cundill psyche.

10

Surviving a Crash

THE BEGINNING OF 1987 brought with it the development of some important relationships for Peter. He had been introduced to Peter Stormonth Darling at a wedding in 1978 and they had become good friends. Darling had spent some years working in Canada for a financial services company set up by Sir Sigmund Warburg, the founder of the eponymous merchant bank, so he and Peter had much in common, both personally and professionally. Sir Sigmund had promoted Darling to the position of vice-chair of Warburgs and given him the task of getting rid of the bank's asset management subsidiary, which Sir Sigmund regarded as a time-wasting distraction.

The result was that in 1979 Darling became the first chief executive of Mercury Asset Management, the independently listed company that under his direction became London's largest fund management company. Darling was immensely well connected in the City of London, generous with his time, and had a great sense of humour and a zest for life. Like Peter, he had a curious mind and took pleasure in knowing some of the zanier characters of the investment world, judging them on the basis of integrity and performance rather than conventionality. He was always intrigued by talented mavericks and he often perceived synergies that others might have missed.

In this vein he had been urging Peter for some time to pay a call on Clarence Dauphinot, the founder of Deltec, a small and very specialized boutique company headquartered in Nassau in the Bahamas. Deltec had a number of niche areas of expertise: Latin America, where it had offices in Buenos Aires and Sao Paulo, and distressed debt, both corporate and sovereign. It had bond trading desks in New York and London and maintained markets in a small way in the securities with which it was involved.

The SEC investigation of Drexel Burnham, which led to the eventual indictment of Michael Milken and demise of its entire "distressed debt" team in Los Angeles, was gathering pace. With its disintegration Peter lost his access to the group that had been his primary source of high quality research in that particular arena of value investment. Peter was reluctant to forego the opportunities that distressed debt markets often afforded and was consequently on the look-out for groups with the same kind of expertise that Drexel had developed. He had been intending for quite a while to visit his friend and client John Templeton in Nassau and, while he was there, he finally arranged to meet up with Dauphinot:

> I had lunch with John Templeton at the Lyford Cay Club and then went back to his office to continue chatting about investments and spiritual matters too. John was open and warm and he asked first-rate questions on the investment front. He finally began to call me Peter, which really meant something to me. Afterwards he drove me over to Deltec, which occupies a rather larger building than Templeton right at the entrance to the Club. Dauphinot is a couple of years younger than John; a bit of a buccaneer – charmingly roguish but with integrity. He understands value and is a player in my distressed stuff. He is close, both professionally and through family, to Al Gordon,

> the saviour of Kidder, and, at the ripe old age of eighty, a marathon runner.

The relationship with Deltec turned out to be long and fruitful and resulted in Peter making some of the most profitable investments of his career in South American sovereign debt.

In the meantime, as 1987 developed stock markets were becoming increasingly over-valued and Peter began to feel that the frenzy was building up into something which might turn out to be more serious than just an ordinary correction. At the beginning of March he had lunch with Jean-François Canton of the Caisse des Dépots, the largest investment institution in Paris, who was an investor in the Value Fund and Peter noted:

> He is as bearish as I am. He told me that Soros has gone short Japan, not something that Soros himself mentioned at our recent meeting but definitely in harmony with my instincts. Canton and I had an excellent exchange – he understands value investment thoroughly. As I see it, with money being recklessly printed, higher inflation and higher interest rates must be just around the corner and so must the likelihood of a real and possibly violent stock market collapse. I have an unpleasant feeling that a tidal wave is preparing to overwhelm the financial system, so in the midst of the euphoria around I'm just planning for survival.

By the time the crash finally happened in October Peter was more than well prepared in the Value Fund, which was holding over 40% of its assets in short term money market instruments. But, as he said at the board meeting in November, this positioning was not the result of a deliberate decision to build up cash because, although he had anticipated a crash, he could not have predicted its exact timing. The enlarged cash position was actually the result of the increasing number of securities in the portfolio that had been attaining prices considerably in excess of book value, consequently qualifying them for an automatic sale unless there were overriding reasons to hold on to them. It was in effect the perfect example of the way the value discipline in action provided a form of inbuilt safety valve.

October 1987 found Peter in Hong Kong,where the crash actually began. The Dow Jones in New York had started to slide during the previous week, down 4.5% on the Wednesday, 3% on Thursday, and another 6% on Friday, with the selling frenzy gathering pace throughout the day, gaining momentum right up to thc closing bell with no sign of a rally.

With the week-end to reflect on the way markets had behaved in the last three days of trading the tension was palpable and traders and investors alike began to lose their nerve. As Peter observed, the carefree mood was instantly wiped out as people spent the normal Hong Kong working Saturday assessing the damage and gloom began to settle on their faces. Personally he was finding it difficult to restrain his glee. In the journal for that day he recorded a quotation from Horace's *Ars Poetica*, one that had been used by Ben Graham himself;

> Many shall be restored that now are fallen, and many shall fall that are now held in honour.

By the time Black Monday dawned, absolute panic began to set in, starting in Hong Kong and spreading like wildfire across international markets; by the close Hong Kong was down 400 points, well over 20%, the Nikkei was down 600, a similar percentage, and the Dow Jones had fallen by an unprecedented 508 points or 22.6% – still the largest-ever single day's decline in its history. These collapses exceeded even the Wall Street crash of 1929 and investors, professional and retail alike, were now simply shell-shocked and terrified. Peter, by contrast, was relaxed and confident, with his pen and calculator poised to focus on the bargains which had already begun to appear and he observed:

> We are relatively well positioned at this juncture. I do not anticipate a total melt-down of the financial system. There appears to be an organized and well structured international approach emerging to cope with the crisis and to inject liquidity rapidly. The Keynesian lessons of the 1930s have been well learnt. But one, nevertheless, does better to keep a low profile, especially when talking to the former optimists. There is too much pain around for there to be any temptation to gloat. But, somehow, the word is out on the street that we have been prescient, both in thought and action, prior to the event and are ready to exploit it to advantage. I suppose that this in itself contributes in a small way to a stabilizing effect, especially in these sorts of markets where buyers are scarce and volumes are thin.
>
> I took calls which were slightly panicky from Deltec and Novelly, I think seeking reassurance as much as anything else and, for the moment, we are perceived as being a safe haven. How long this view will last is a matter for conjecture. Will we begin to see a wave of buying of the Value Fund, or will redemptions, to support margin calls elsewhere, counter-balance this? Only time will tell.

As the days went on Peter became increasingly impressed by the steady-handed, pragmatic approach being exhibited by most of the authorities around the world. They were not just offering platitudinous reassurance but were backing up their confident statements on the economy and interest rates by providing very substantial liquidity to drive rates down and prevent economic activity from stalling. Firm action was being taken by imposing day limits on the percentage falls on the world's stock exchanges and on individual securities that would be permissible before trading was automatically suspended, and this had the effect of making the procedure of short selling much more dangerous, because it was impossible to gauge with any certainty at what point, after a suspension, trading might be resumed, giving the short seller the opportunity to cover his position. In the extremely volatile conditions that obtained such uncertainty represented a "risk too far" for many of the usual short operators. In Hong Kong the authorities went even further:

> They have shut the exchange for three days until Monday – a wise move on balance. As I have watched events unfold I have come to the conclusion that computers actually don't do much more than make it quicker for investors to react to information. The problem is that having the information in its raw state on a second by second basis is not at all the same thing as interpreting and understanding its implications, and this applies in rising markets as well as falling ones. Spur of the moment reactions to partially digested information are, more often than not, disastrous. My impressions of the last week are that most people in shock need to share their gloom and doom, to reassure themselves that they are not out there on their own, and so it feeds on itself.
>
> The authorities are continuing to do the right things internationally, with the notable exception of Japan, which appears to be sweeping every problem under the table. If and when this is uncovered, the real massacre will begin. We will, of course, be hurt, but there will be extraordinary opportunities as a result

and we can take advantage. I am concerned over the credit worthiness of some of the investment bankers and dealers. Even so, while my moral instincts cry punishment to the perpetrators of unholy levels of security prices, my professional instincts yell, "Thank God for them, where would we be without them?"

Peter's optimism was fully justified in terms of the response of the global economy to the flood of liquidity that had been injected. However it was fortunate that his investment strategy had been thoroughly planned well in advance, because the window of opportunity for bargain hunting turned out to be extremely short. Over the month of October the Dow Jones had fallen by 23%, Toronto by 25%, and Hong Kong by a vertiginous 45%, but the turn-around was equally like a whiplash, as the world's economies showed no sign whatever of stalling, so that by the end of the year the Dow Jones had halved its losses to just 12% and Toronto had completely recovered, being merely flat for the year. Peter had managed to repurchase some of the positions sold earlier in the spring and summer, notably Cliffs and Hanna Mining, and the fund actually ended the year up by 13%, which was impressive by contrast with both the indices and the mutual fund industry in general. However, the concern that margin calls, occasioned by losses incurred elsewhere by investors, might lead to redemptions from the Value Fund proved to be all too real and the fund's capital actually declined year on year by $15 million in spite of the appreciation.

Although this was not entirely unexpected, Peter was disappointed. His caution and discipline had been more than vindicated but, for the moment, it seemed that investors simply did not care. The financial press, nevertheless, were hot on his trail. Articles about him began to appear with increasing frequency and he was much in demand to give interviews. There was one that he particularly relished from

BC Business in February 1988 entitled "Chronicle of a Cheapskate," where he was described as "a contrarian fund manager extraordinaire with the instincts of a vulture" and which included two pithy quotations:

> Sooner or later the market will do what it has to do to prove the majority wrong.

And:

> My best advice to individual investors can readily be summed up in two closely linked precepts. Be patient and don't be greedy.

As the year progressed and the performance of the fund continued to move ahead, investors did start to pay attention and the subscription checks began to roll in. By the end of the year the Value Fund had appreciated by 19% but funds under management had risen by 33%. Remarkably, this had been achieved while consistently holding 40% in cash and short term instruments. In addition to the inflow of investor funds, Peter had been substantially reducing the commitment to US markets. But there was no question of his simply sitting around twiddling his thumbs waiting for North America to get cheaper. Europe, where the pickup after the 1987 crash had been much more muted, particularly in the German market, was beckoning.

The bottom line of the attraction of German stocks was Peter's discovery of an accounting anomaly. German companies almost without exception overstated their liabilities so that in some cases as much as 50% of what was presented as long term debt in the accounts was in fact equity. Nor was there any need to delve into obscure or even second tier companies to find this value: it was true of the bluest of the blue chips and so Siemens, BASF, Volkswagen, and, most importantly, Deutsche Bank all turned out to be net-nets and were immediately added to the overseas investment portfolio. In the case of Deutsche Bank, its extensive proprietary investment portfolio, when valued at market, was equivalent to the total value of shareholders' equity, so you were paying nothing for the bank itself. Peter described the discovery in his own colourful fashion:

> Every time I kicked over a rock I'd wind up finding gold rather than moss underneath.

In 1988 the Cundill Conference was to be held in New York to coincide with Peter's fiftieth birthday. He had secured a star speaker who was deliberately chosen to underline the fact that European markets were very much on the agenda. At the beginning of October Peter had lunch in London with Lord Jenkins of Hillhead. Jenkins had been a distinguished member of the British Cabinet, holder of two of the great offices of state as Chancellor of the Exchequer and Home Secretary. He had been deputy leader of the Labour Party and a founder member of the breakaway Social Democratic Party. In spite of his impeccable working-class background, from a coal-mining town in North Wales, he had been wittily characterized by British Prime Minister Harold Wilson as "more of a socialite than a socialist."

Jenkins had in fact made the transition, generally regarded as impossible in Britain, of casting off his proletarian roots and becoming a prominent establishment figure. The process had probably been facilitated by his having a strong epicurean streak with a particular fondness for fine wines, especially grand cru claret. He had a first-rate mind and was a much admired political biographer, most famously of

Roosevelt and Winston Churchill, and he became, until his death in 2003, a popular and successful chancellor of Oxford University. The lunch was a convivial one:

> Jenkins was courteous and cordial, an excellent conversationalist and good raconteur with a constant glint of humour in his eye and a fine sense of irony. I had no impression that he had any particular interest in me personally, except possibly as a donor to the university, although as Chancellor of the Exchequer he must have got to know everyone of importance in the world of finance on the national and international stage. However, knowing doesn't necessarily mean liking, but I have no doubt at all that he will do a great job as a conference speaker. In particular, as ex-president of the European Commission and the man directly responsible for the negotiations that led to the formation of the common currency, he is well placed to make the case for it to a moderately sceptical audience.

Jenkins lived up to Peter's expectations:

> Roy Jenkins led off in the library of the Metropolitan Club on the topic of the European Community on which, as the first-ever president of the European Commission, he is considered to be something of an authority. He was humorous, articulate, and informative, delivering stylish epigrams in a thoroughly patrician manner that was still not in the least patronizing. His address was very well received, as was Sydney Grierson on Russian/US relations during lunch and in the afternoon Ed Altman [Max Heine Professor of Finance at the Stern Business School, NYU] took the session on Chapter XI, running it as though it were a graduate seminar, which was wonderful.

There was a fine dinner at Maxim's that evening attended by all the speakers, at which Jenkins clearly enjoyed himself. Peter himself was in "no martini mode" in reserve for "Pete's Morning" at 9 am the next day. It was a compelling performance:

> Stu Shapiro complimented me, he said I was "getting dangerous" and he doesn't offer praise lightly. As lunch was finishing Gowan [then chair of the Value Fund] gave an impromptu speech that resulted in a standing ovation for me and then he delayed the board meeting until all the wives arrived. The board presented me with a tropical outfit and a trip to Mount Everest for next spring. I was completely overwhelmed and I walked back to the Surrey with the adrenalin pumping.

Someone took the trouble to transcribe at least part of Peter's address:

> On the subject of the "fallen angels" of stock markets that occupy so much of our detective work as value investors, I try to keep in mind Oscar Wilde's comment that "saints always have a past and sinners always have a future," so no investment should be ruled out simply on the basis of past history. We focus on liquidation analysis and liquidation analysis alone.
>
> The Japanese value politeness, persistence, dedication, and memory more than inventiveness. But in any case we hold a couple of Japanese stocks because Japan's just too big to ignore and we want to be polite.
>
> To a Canadian like me almost all stocks in the world are by definition foreign and, given the dearth of bargains in North America today, it pays to search for them everywhere. For years, every November, when it would get rainy in Vancouver,

I would up sticks and go visit the worst stock market over the first eleven months of the year. For my sins that first year I ended up in Sweden, where in late November it's even darker and bleaker than Vancouver. But the practice served me well on that occasion and has continued to do so.

I've thought a lot over the years about the everlasting obsession with trying to predict where markets will go at any particular juncture, not least since last year's crash when it was our value disciplines that kept us out of trouble, holding oodles of cash. We believed that a correction of some magnitude was highly probable but we had no idea when it would happen. So, for what it's worth, here's my present thought on the subject – maybe not my final thought, who knows? Synchronicity begins where pure chance ends, with one event leading to another, like a chain reaction, but all brought about by the initial event which cannot be predicted or explained. In other words – don't waste your time. Just have patience and make sure you're confident about the margin of safety in each investment.

11

Distressed Corporate Securities and Defaulted Sovereign Debt

DISTRESSED CORPORATE DEBT and the debt of companies under Chapter XI bankruptcy protection, or its equivalent outside the United States, was a field with which Peter was already thoroughly familiar and it had provided him with some stellar returns in the 1980s, especially in the real estate sector with Daon and NuWest. It fitted perfectly into his Graham and Dodd framework because the departure point in researching distressed corporate debt is always the balance sheet. What one needs to determine is whether, as the re-organization, or the liquidation, proceeds in an orderly fashion rather than a panic sale, the sum of the parts, or the rump of the business, is worth more than the debt at its discounted price. Will the company be in a position to pay a sufficient redemption price in a negotiated settlement with the bondholders to make the investment worthwhile?

The second part of the procedure in establishing the existence of the essential margin of safety is the small print in each trust indenture; sometimes overlooked by those buying distressed debt. This is particularly important where a company has issued a whole series of different instruments because they will not all necessarily rank on equal terms in the creditors' pecking order. A mistake over this can prove very expensive indeed, but it is the sort of minefield that Peter has always thoroughly enjoyed.

The last element in the analytical equation is time, and in that final analysis it is the one aspect that has to be a matter of judgement and experience, even if bolstered by expert outside opinion. Clearly, the more quickly a settlement can be reached, the higher the return is likely to be, but the negotiations are rarely absolutely straightforward and it is essential to temper impatience so as not to settle for too little but at the same time not to be so greedy as to cause the negotiations to become bogged down. And, especially in the case of Chapter XI protection, one needs to be conscious of the fact that whatever is agreed between the negotiating parties will have to be presented to the Court, which will always need to be persuaded that the proposed settlement is fair to all parties, not just those who can afford legal representation.

The perfect illustration of the vital importance of time was a lesson that Peter learned through LTV Corporation, which had become one of the United States' largest steel producers after its acquisition of Republic Steel in 1984. The timing of this acquisition could not have been worse as the American steel market was almost immediately inundated with inexpensive imported steel from ultramodern plants in Japan, Europe, and Canada, which quickly captured 30% of the domestic market. Attempts to modernize LTV and improve productivity met with small success and the debt incurred by the investment, which at the time was costing 15% to service, bled the company white. A pension fund shortfall forced it into bankruptcy under Chapter XI in the middle of 1986.

Enter the Cundill Value Fund. Peter's analysis of the balance sheet showed, perfectly correctly, that LTV was sitting on some very valuable real estate that, on its own, was sufficient to assure the company's survival and provide for a handsome return on the debt if and when it emerged from bankruptcy. However what Peter failed to appreciate were the complexities that would be involved in the negotiations, which were complicated by the labour unions and the question of the pension fund shortfall. The experience was anything but the joyride anticipated. Months dragged into years and it was not until the middle of 1993 that LTV finally came out of bankruptcy protection after one of the longest and most complicated bankruptcy cases in American corporate history.

It was a big position in the Value Fund and, while it was not in the end a loss in absolute terms, on the basis of the "time value" of money, the emotional wear and tear that it caused, and the man-hours wasted, it was a dismal result and had dragged down performance. The lesson, however, was thoroughly absorbed and Peter acknowledged that patience and stubbornness are not necessarily the same things, although an element of stubbornness has to be an essential attribute of all successful value investors. What provides the vital balance is a willingness to reanalyse and reappraise all assumptions and calculations throughout the process.

In the Graham and Dodd sense there are several additional characteristics of distressed debt that, in Peter's view, render it compatible with the framework. The rating system operated by agencies such as Moody's and Standard and Poor's is applied to every issue of corporate bonds in the world and there is a clear divide between what is classified as investment grade and what is not. If a bond is of investment grade it is qualified for inclusion in the portfolios of pension funds, conservative bond funds, and low-risk managed client portfolios. Bonds below investment grade can, for the most part, be owned only by specialist institutions.

The result is that as soon as a company goes into default, or Chapter XI bankruptcy protection, its corporate bonds drop onto the bottom rung of the non-investment grade group. In the case of many investing institutions this means that they are obliged by statute to sell them, if they can, whether they like it or not. Even institutions that may not actually be obliged to sell may do so anyway to avoid the embarrassment of having an obvious carbuncle in their portfolio. In consequence the price decline of bonds in these circumstances is usually precipitous and very often totally unrelated to any realistic estimate of intrinsic value. At this stage there was usually a predatory glint in Peter's eye – a look that his wife came to recognize instantly – once famously remarking in public: "You must be happy. You're wearing your vulture's smile."

Another feature of distressed debt that Peter was quick to recognize is that its trading price bears practically no correlation to the general direction of either the stock market or the bond market. It is almost entirely determined by the condition of the company alone. The only external factor that may have an influence is the overall direction of interest rates but, unless there are extreme changes, even this seems to have little impact. The result is that such investments provide a lot of what is technically referred to in a portfolio as Alpha, a measure of the risk-adjusted return on any investment. Such a measure tries to determine whether the return on an investment is sufficient to justify the exposure. Clearly, if one can eliminate most of the stock and bond market risk, the answer is more likely to be yes.

The final aspect of distressed debt that Peter was early in appreciating was that once the bad news is out and the price has fallen, if the analysis demonstrates to one's satisfaction that the company is going to survive, or that it can sell off enough valuable assets to settle with its creditors at an appealing level in relation to the price at which the debt can be purchased, then the downside risk is minimal. The "x factor" is "the time value of money." In simple terms this means that the longer one is obliged to hold an investment, the higher the end return needs to be to justify it – 10% in a month is a better return than 100% in two years. However, the returns on distressed debt, if the analysis is correct, will be comparable to the returns on a successful equity portfolio and not a conventional bond portfolio.

Sovereign debt is perhaps harder to rationalize within the Graham and Dodd framework. Strictly speaking, sovereign nations do not have readily analysable balance sheets, but they do have assets: mineral wealth, manufacturing capacity, a labour force, and an ability to levy taxes. Above all, without exception, from time to time they need to borrow funds on both domestic and international markets and this means that permanently alienating lenders is not a viable long-term strategy.

The reality of this constraint is amply illustrated in some startling historical statistics. Between 1800 and 1992 seventy-two countries have defaulted 162 times between them, but there have only been 14 instances in which the debt has not eventually been rescheduled and, even among those 14, it is not impossible that it may yet be. This, of course, does not mean that such debts have been repaid in full – far from it – but invariably the rescheduling has been at a level substantially above the lowest prices at which these obligations could have been acquired during the default period.

Conventional investors do not often appreciate the risk, whether political or economic, that may be involved in the purchase of sovereign debt on the primary markets or at issue price, and this is especially so in the case of "emerging markets." To some extent this is reflected in the credit rating attached to each sovereign issuer, but the rating differentials are often not reflected adequately in the yield differentials in the real market place. This has been well illustrated in the case of Greek sovereign debt in recent months, where the risk could fairly be regarded as both political and economic. The spread between Greek bonds and the German bund markets never exceeded 400 basis points (4%), although the risk associated with the potential of a Greek default by comparison with that of a German default was, and is, obviously immeasurably greater and the margin of safety negligible, or at least unquantifiable. If one imagines what the result of an actual Greek default might be on its outstanding international debt, it is not hard to envisage the possibility of a 30% decline in traded value and conceivably much more than that.

However, if such a default occurred and the market in Greek bonds declined to 70 cents on the Euro, even on a purely historical basis the risk-reward ratio would have swung markedly in favour of the investor. The relevance of all this may seem decidedly obscure in relation to Peter's thinking on the subject of sovereign credit markets in the early 1990s, but it actually lies at the core of why he felt that such investments did not in fact represent a conflict within a Graham and Dodd–based value framework.

A case in point is Panamanian debt. Throughout the 1970s and at the very beginning of the 1980s Panama was regarded by the United States as a favoured nation with whom it was prepared to do business and as an ally in the region. However by 1985 the lawless regime of General Manuel Noriega, which was implicated in political murder and drug trafficking, had alienated the United States' administration, with the result that aid was withdrawn. This, combined with the political turmoil, seriously weakened the economy, impairing the country's ability to service its outstanding debt.

Relations continued to worsen as the charges against Noriega became more serious; the last straw was a regime-inspired attack on the US Embassy in Panama City, which resulted in some loss of American lives. President Reagan then froze all Panamanian assets in US banks and suspended payments on the use of the canal. Panama's debt default followed swiftly in early 1988 and was followed by political and economic chaos. By 1989 the situation had become so serious that

US troops took control of the Panama Canal, although in theory it was obligated by an earlier treaty to hand over full title to Panama on 1 January 1990. Just before Christmas the United States invaded Panama, ousted Noriega, and restored order to the stricken city.

Both Peter and the Deltec people had been watching these developments with increasing interest. Peter had noted Noriega's taking refuge in the Vatican Embassy in his journal that Christmas Eve. In the aftermath of the invasion Panamanian debt prices fell even more steeply and Peter set to work to look at the situation in detail from an economic standpoint. What emerged from his analysis over the next few months was startling and mouth-watering. The cash assets belonging to Panama that were frozen in US banks equated approximately to its outstanding defaulted obligations. With order re-established the economy was beginning to thrive once more and there was every reason to suppose that the US Government would move to restore a properly elected democratic administration in Panama as soon as possible and, by implication, a legitimate, recognized independent Panamanian government would be fully entitled to expect conformity with the treaty terms relating to the control and administration of the Panama Canal, which had been abrogated at the time of the invasion.

In Peter's judgement this constituted a very considerable and solid margin of safety. In effect one would be buying cash at a discount and getting the canal and the Panamanian economy for nothing. If ever there were a good example of the principle of "buying a dollar for 40 cents" – a phrase that was already a motto for the Cundill Value Fund – this was it. With the Republic of Panama dollar-denominated debt trading at just over 50 cents by early 1992, Peter was more than a little tempted but the selling pressure was still intense and so he held off, remarking:

Markets can be overvalued and still keep on getting more expensive for quite a while, or they can be undervalued and keep getting cheaper, which is why investing is an art form, not an exact science.

However, he did not have long to wait. By December 1992 Panama's dollar-denominated debt had fallen to below 35 cents and Peter stepped in. He was able to accumulate his position at an average price of 39 cents. It was sold in May 1995 with a gain of 121% or 61% annualized; a little early but still a very handsome return.

Panama was not the first of Peter's ventures into defaulted sovereign debt. In early 1990 he had paid an extensive visit to South America, travelling to Brazil, Argentina, and Ecuador. The reason behind the tour was that in March 1989 the United States had sponsored the creation of Brady Bonds in order to permit a large number of Latin American countries who had defaulted in the 1980s to convert their obligations (mostly in the form of syndicated bank loans) into a variety of these new bonds – the Brady's, brainchild of US Treasury Secretary Nicholas Brady.

The US administration had come to realize that, as a result of the defaults, the availability of credit to these developing countries had all but dried up and this was having a seriously depressive effect on their growth, generating high unemployment and "stagflation." This in turn was creating a violent and unstable political and social environment that was fertile ground for extremism and the more dangerous forms of criminality, especially in the area of drugs, where export trafficking was a matter of growing concern to the United States.

The most important and innovative feature of the Brady Bonds was that they created a mechanism through which commercial banks who had lent to the defaulters were able to exchange their virtually illiquid claims (the syndicated bank loans) for marketable securities and thus remove these non-performing "assets" from their balance sheets. By contrast with the defaulted claims, Brady Bonds were actively traded and highly liquid.

The attraction for the defaulting countries was that the negotiations relating to the issue of the Brady Bonds, almost without exception, resulted in a significant discount on the quantum of the original loan, on top of which closure on these overhanging debts meant that a reopening of access to international credit was possible once more. Like all good deals, there was a lot to be gained on both sides.

The South American visit turned out to be the first step in a long and profitable investment journey, particularly in relation to Ecuador, and it is worthwhile to quote extensively from Peter's investment notebooks to illustrate just how thorough his approach was and how well it was attuned to the Graham and Dodd style of balance sheet analysis:

> ECUADOREAN BANK DEBT
>
> Based on the refinancing recently agreed between Costa Rica and its commercial banking creditors, we ought seriously to consider buying Ecuadorean debt at its current levels of around 17.5 cents on the dollar. The Costa Rican debt appreciated by over 60% in barely four months on the basis of the Brady Bond terms and, following my visit to Ecuador, I believe that there is a high probability that it too will be able to negotiate a similar deal on its $5.5 billion of syndicated bank loans. The time frame may be slightly longer but the absolute return is likely to be very similar.
>
> This is the nub of it. Costa Rica paid 16 cents in cash on 60% of its loans, plus 16 cents cash on the accrued interest. The 40% balance of the loans was exchanged for 20 year bonds carrying a coupon of 6.25% and these bonds are now

trading at 40 cents. The accrued interest portion of this tranche was paid in cash in full as to 20 % and the rest in 15 year floating rate notes paying LIBOR. These are presently trading at 50 cents. If we had paid top dollar for a slice of these debts prior to the deal the cost would have been 20 cents, as against the present market value of the package of 32 cents – a 60% return.

How do the two countries compare? The debt to GNP ratio of the two countries is almost identical, Ecuador's debt service cost ratio slightly lower. Both are heavily dependent on agricultural exports, but there is one significant difference – CR is an importer of oil and Ecuador is a member of OPEC, has about 400,000 bbls of production, and is an exporter – oil revenues representing just over 40% of total exports. Its proven reserves are 1.5 billion bbls. On the fiscal front Ecuador also enjoys an advantage in running a budget surplus (ex debt service) of 2.0% of GNP.

What about the politics? Ecuador's population is just over 10 million and it returned to democracy in 1984 with Febres, a Christian Democrat, as president. He tried to implement an austerity program to tackle inflation and create a basis for economic growth. This was unpopular, but the program was not actually derailed until the earthquake in 1988, which upset oil production and led to the moratorium on interest payments. The whole unfortunate coincidence of events beyond the government's control led to Febres's defeat in the 1988 election, won by Boria of the moderate centrist left. He is in power until 1992 and has taken important steps, including significant tax reforms, towards re-establishing Ecuador as a fully fledged member of the international community. A standby financing has been provided by the IMF and is due to expire and be renegotiated next February. Commencing discussions on the terms of a Brady package on its external debt would obviously do Ecuador no harm with the IMF!

Peter made his first purchases of Ecuadorean debt in November 1992 at 20 cents. His average price was just under 34 cents. The last stub of the position was sold in April 1995. The annualized return was 42%. Events had turned out exactly as Peter had anticipated after his visit.

The experiments in Panamanian and Ecuadorean debt were only the beginning. Between 1992 and 2000 Peter bought and sold them a number of times. The gains were over $20 million and the average annualized returns well over 70%.

However, there is a fascinating footnote to Peter's engagement with distressed debt. One of the common characteristics of the greatest investors seems to be boundless curiosity. I shall try, as I sum up at the end of this account, to enumerate some of the others. Peter's personal curiosity is in no sense confined to purely investment matters, even though these are central to his life. One Sunday morning in early 1990, as he was scanning the newspapers over a leisurely and substantial English breakfast, he noticed that Bonhams, London's third major auction house, was holding a sale of bankrupt bonds from the collection of the Corporation of Foreign Bond Holders. Peter was immediately intrigued.

His investigation revealed that the CFBH had been set up in 1868 to protect the interests of British investors in foreign bonds anywhere in the world and, on their behalf, to pursue debt issuers in default. It had done this with considerable success for 120 years but, as debt renegotiation became more complex and litigation ever more costly, in 1988 it had itself gone into liquidation. What Bonhams was selling off was a range of the bonds that CFBH had collected over the years, including Russian and Chinese railway debentures.

However, what particularly caught Peter's attention was a large lot ($300,000 nominal) of State of Mississippi bonds issued in 1838. Needless to say Bonhams was not selling the bonds as an investment in the financial sense. They are in fact highly decorative, as well as being fascinating from a historical point of view. But Peter's mind was already beginning to move in several different directions.

As he quickly discovered, there was a plethora of information available. Mississippi had issued approximately $7 million of these bonds in the 1830s to fund the foundation of two banks in the state – the Union Bank and the Planters' Bank – both of which, by the end of the decade, had gone spectacularly bankrupt through a combination of reckless investment and corruption, events that perhaps did not entirely surprise the bondholders. What did take them by surprise was that after the fifth semi-annual coupon payment on these bonds Mississippi stopped paying and then in 1841 entirely repudiated the debt. The sense of injury, even outrage, was widespread, as the bonds had been marketed internationally, to some extent in Paris and Berlin but particularly in the City of London, where the impression had been cultivated that the southern State of Mississippi was run by gentlemen whose word was as good as their bond. It was a rude awakening and to add insult to injury the Mississippi legislature held a referendum in which the electorate, all of them, of course, taxpayers, voted with unsurprising unanimity not to honour the debt.

As soon as the CFBH was constituted it took up the cudgels and put in a new demand for a settlement from Mississippi, expressing the view that the repudiation and the referendum were unconstitutional. After some head scratching the state legislature passed another resolution, which read equally uncompromisingly: "The State shall not assume, redeem, secure or pay any indebtedness claim to be due by The State of Mississippi, to any person, association or corporation whatsoever, claiming the same as owners, holders or assignees, of any bond or bonds known as the Union Bank bonds, or Planters' Bank bonds."

In the light of the parlous condition of Mississippi's finances in the aftermath of the Civil War, the CFBH decided that the matter was probably not worth pursuing in the courts. However it was not forgotten and remained on their "agenda." In 1913 Mississippi once more attempted to tap international credit markets and the CFBH wrote an open letter to the *New York Times* correcting an assertion in that newspaper that the State of Mississippi's credit had always been in good standing. "Between 1831 and 1838, Mississippi borrowed $7 million, for which she obtained full value and the proceeds of which were invested in the Planters' and Union Banks. As long as the banks were commercially successful the State paid her debt to the holders of the bonds. But when bad times came and the banks failed Mississippi suspended payments, and has since consistently refused to recognize its defaulted obligation."

They never let up and by the time the CFBH was wound up 120 years later the Mississippi bonds had become notorious as the oldest unpaid debt on record. But it is a salutary reflection for others who might contemplate default and refusal to negotiate that, to this day, Mississippi remains unable to access credit on the London financial markets and that, to all intents and purposes, means that international financial markets are closed to it, the only state in the Union of which this is true, despite there having been a number of other previous state defaulters.*

---

*http://notesfromthebartender.wordpress.com/2010/02/13/the-dangers-of-sovereign-debt]

Peter put in a bid for the Bonhams' lot for his personal account and bought it for just under £7,000. To begin with he simply had some framed and hung around his office in London and in Vancouver and he gave a few away to friends and colleagues whom he thought might also enjoy them. But the idea that it might be worthwhile to take a tilt at Mississippi in the courts continued to simmer. Even if it were unsuccessful, as it might well prove to be, the exercise would almost certainly be instructive and entertaining.

In 1992 he took the plunge and quickly discovered that he was not alone in the idea – two other suits had already been filed: one by a group of fifteen European bondholders and the other by three US holders. It made sense to consolidate the suits in the first legal action that had been mounted against Mississippi on the issue, although there had been plenty of attempts at moral suasion, including, notably, those by the poet William Wordsworth, Queen Isabella II of Spain, and one of the ruling princes of the House of Monaco.

Peter's own portion of the suit claimed for repayment of principal ($300,000) in full plus 154 years of coupon at 5%, plus compound interest thereon. It is an interesting reflection on the power of compound interest over long periods of time that the value of that claim, if it had been met in full, was just short of $1.2 billion. The suit named as defendants the state of Mississippi, Governor Kirk Fordyce, Treasurer Marshall Bennett, and Attorney General Michael Moore.

Not surprisingly, the state took it seriously. In substance the suit alleged that the 1875 amendment to the constitution violated both the Mississippi and the US constitutions and that the ban on repayment was an "unconstitutional impairment of the contract by the state of Mississippi," violating numerous additional sections of the US Constitution, including the limitations on state powers, the ban on the taking of property without compensation, and the due process and equal protection clauses in the 14th amendment. It also charged that the nonpayment violated a friendship treaty of 1794 between the United States and Great Britain.

All of this was very hard to refute and a Chancery Court judge in Hinds County unequivocally declared that the 1875 Mississippi State Legislature's amendment was unconstitutional but, unfortunately, that a seven-year statute of limitations law that had been passed by the state in 1873 applied to the bonds, pre-empting the law suit.

Curiously enough, both plaintiffs and defendants appealed. The state disliked the unconstitutionality ruling and Peter's group obviously wanted the statute of limitations lifted. The appeal failed on both counts, although the moral victory was undoubtedly in favour of the bondholder group and did nothing to enhance or retrieve the financial reputation of Mississippi. Today the bonds are worth about $300 apiece, making Peter's original £7,000 investment worth about £30,000. That, of course, does not constitute a profit after the legal expenses, but the bonds continue to make a charming and interesting present.*

*http://www.highbeam.com 1995 Source Media Inc

12

Dealing with Adversity

AT THE END OF 1989 the Value Fund posted its fifteenth year of unbroken positive returns, gaining a respectable 10%. Although this was less than the Dow Jones or the TSE, it still firmly supported the fund's remarkable fifteen-year compound growth record of 22%. Peter was disappointed but not despondent and the coming year seemed to hold promise. The worst of the SEC investigation of Drexel Burnham now appeared to be over, so that there was good reason to expect an improvement in the high yield market, and Westar, the fund's largest and most problematic position, looked as though it would be resolved profitably by the intervention of Sam Belzberg.

From Peter's perspective the uncertainties in the political world held the promise of opportunity, rather than spelling disaster. His overall mood comes across in the journal entry for Christmas Day:

> Noriega, the Panamanian tyrant, is hiding out in, of all places, the Vatican Embassy after the US invasion; Ceausescu of Romania and his wife have been summarily executed, demonstrating that failed communist dictators cannot expect to be immune from the consequences of their tyranny; and Bernstein conducted a Christmas performance of Beethoven's Ninth at the

Schauspielhaus in East Berlin. The orchestra was composed of players from the four allied powers that governed the city after the war and from East and West Germany. At the end of the performance he recited Schiller's "Ode to Joy,"

"... All men become brothers
Under the sway of thy gentle wings."

Is this order or chaos? Here at home we exchanged presents, warmth, and love, mine were *Churchill, The Last Lion* by William Manchester and a multitude of stuff from "Liar's Poker."

On New Year's day Peter undertook his customary exercise in critical analysis of the year's investment performance and he prefaced it with this comment:

Just as many smart people fail in the investment business as stupid ones. Intellectually active people are particularly attracted to elegant concepts, which can have the effect of distracting them from the simpler, more fundamental, truths.

What were last year's mistakes – Southmark, Crazy Eddie, Japanese Warrants, Westar, and BC Capital? Why – in BCC I broke my own rules in terms of debt. I was so fascinated by the cash flow that I overlooked the high debt. Listening to poor advice and acting on it? How does one reduce the margin of error while recognizing that investments do, of course, go down as well as up? The answers are not absolutely clear cut but they certainly include refusing to compromise by subtly changing a question so that it shapes the answer one is looking for, and continually reappraising the research approach, constantly revisiting and rechecking the detail.

What were last year's winners – Public Service of New Jersey and Deutsche Bank? Why? – I usually had the file myself, I started with a small position and stayed that way until I was completely satisfied with every detail.

And, indeed, the year began well. Peter had lunch at the Savoy Hotel in London with his great Drexel friend Peter Ackerman where they philosophized and shared their views on the investment climate without restraint. He learnt that Ackerman had emerged from the whole Milken scandal unscathed, having been fully investigated and vindicated.

A few days later he attended a High Yield investment conference in New York sponsored by the Chartered Financial Analysts Association. There was a presentation by Ed Altman, who had so impressed Peter as a speaker at the Cundill Conference the year before. Altman maintained that the worst of the investigatory fall-out, or as he put it "witch hunt," was over and that one could, therefore, concentrate primarily on values. This view, put forward by such a distinguished investment academic, was naturally music to Peter's ears and he caught a flight to Nassau to participate in a Deltec board meeting in an optimistic frame of mind.

Ran 7 ½ miles along the beach in bare feet – lovely sensation of freedom – and then headed for the Lyford Cay Club for the meeting. Senior Latinos were there in full force, Colombia, Chile, Mexico, Argentina, Brazil, and Venezuela along with the Taurus people, Henley, and the Kuwait Investment Office, all of them shareholders of Deltec. After lunch Enrique Holmberg,

Deltec's man in Buenos Aires, made an emotional but cogent speech about Argentina which was compelling enough for me to take a serious look at the US dollar denominated sovereign debt.

After the meeting I went over to visit with John Templeton, whom I see as something of a mentor. He is extraordinary in the breadth of his skills and interests and yet he can be so dry and seemingly humourless, even egotistical and mean-minded. He is a highly complex personality – for all the beaming patriarchal smile – and yet I always have to acknowledge that he has given me enormous help not just in financial matters but in spiritual ways too. Somchow I still can't imagine having a warm dinner with him where the reserve is abandoned. Maybe it will happen one day."

When Peter got back to London there was a copy of *Barron's International* waiting for him. Not only was he in it but his picture was on the front cover. Inside there were more photographs and a full feature article by Alan Abelson, a highly regarded financial journalist, and it was couched in the most flattering terms. Nevertheless a niggling sense of unease was beginning to creep over Peter. The Japanese economy looked weak and unstable, but the stock market, though volatile and massively overvalued by every sound statistical measure, was not showing much sign of cracking and the Nikkei put options in the Value Fund, which had been being rolled over continuously at a loss since March 1987, were proving to be an expensive drag on the performance.

Peter himself was utterly convinced that the vast majority of Japanese securities were by then grotesquely out of line, trading at prices that could only be justified if predicated upon unsustainably high growth rates. In the end he was to be proved absolutely correct, but in the meantime the relentlessly recurring quarterly decision as to whether or not to renew the puts was weighing on him and he had the feeling that his determination to see it through to the conclusion that he was anticipating was not fully supported internally, especially by his old friend Brian McDermott, and he found this uncomfortable.

Peter had brought McDermott into Peter Cundill and Associates as president, to act as resident administrator, run the operational side of the business from the Vancouver office, and take charge of marketing, leaving him free to concentrate on the investment side from his London base. The journal expresses something of this unease:

> Last night I was anticipating the outcome of the Japanese stock market. I dreamt that the Nikkei fell by a thousand points. In fact it was up 1,450 – the second best day in its history. You must stop this short term anticipation stuff. If you've done the numbers and are satisfied with them and the principle is right, you just have to grit your teeth and be patient.

This was easier said than done, as is clear from the next day's journal entry:

> Tokyo was down a thousand points today – maybe particularly significant as this was the last trading day of the year. I'm going through a period of shocks professionally, particularly in our real-estate stocks, but having these Nikkei puts and Westar as well is worrying, even though I am convinced that all three are right. But you have always to remember that you constantly need to challenge other people's assumptions. Being out on a limb, alone and appearing to be wrong is just part of the territory of value investment.

For Peter, spending Easter with friends in Yorkshire turned out to be the last appearance of a positive attitude of mind for some time. The issue of the performance of the Value Fund was weighing on him and had begun to raise the spectre of self-doubt. At board level, among the old guard, there were no doubters, but within the company itself, whose staff was dependent on the results every year to support the generous bonus culture that had always prevailed, Peter was aware of a degree of unease. The week after Easter his confidence in his own judgement was further shaken by a visit from Peter Ackerman with the news that Michael Milken had finally decided to plead guilty to a number of serious charges. It seemed to spell the end of an era.

The annual general meeting of the Value Fund in Toronto in June was well attended, with a considerable contingent of investment advisors from the Bay Street brokerage community who listened attentively as Peter addressed the audience for nearly three hours, reiterating Graham and Dodd principles and preaching the necessity of patience. To Peter's ears the applause seemed more restrained than usual.

He had lunch in New York with Stuart Shapiro, who regaled him with disturbing anecdotes about the Manhattan real estate market as well as a very negative assessment of the situation in US credit and securities markets. As they walked along Madison Avenue together there were a number of boarded-up shop fronts that seemed to confirm the other anecdotal evidence. The next day Peter recorded his reaction:

> The end of June numbers were not distinguished though not that bad. I keep coming back to the view that credit conditions have deteriorated so badly and so fast that even more cash may be in order. I was on the phone all day selling things. I have made a judgement to get to over 50% in cash and to increase the Japanese short positions. If markets go down I'll go more

into distressed securities both sovereign and corporate when the sell off is overdone. This is a very significant professional decision. It could change my career. Well, off we go!

In the event he simply gritted his teeth over the Nikkei puts and kept on going, ignoring the pressures to cut and run. As he put it himself in an interview years later:

> I almost stopped selling Japan short in the last quarter of 1989 because I couldn't stand it anymore. But intellectually I was convinced that I was right and so I carried on and then in the first quarter of 1990 the Japanese market fell by 25% in eight weeks and I made back everything I'd given away since 1987 plus a good deal more. But I tell you statistical overvaluation is a funny thing – it can go on for a very long time, far beyond the limits of rationality, and it is a problem for the value investor in two ways: it can tempt one to compromise standards on the buy side and it may lure one into selling things far too early. I have less of a problem with the selling temptation because I have always loved cash – if you've got lots of it you will never have to pass up a great opportunity.

Under pressure, however, Peter did make one concession that he was to regret. He sold the Value Fund's largest position in Westar Group Ltd at a thumping loss. The company had been formed in 1978 to privatize various Crown-owned assets and it had gone public at $6.00 per share a year later amid the fanfare of enthusiastic stockbrokers' reports – the largest ever Canadian equity issue at that date. Over the following decade it had made a series of ill-judged and expensive energy acquisitions largely financed by a growing mountain of debt. The share price had collapsed, leaving thousands of small investors feeling bewildered and betrayed. By the time the share price hit $2.00 it popped up on Peter's radar screen and indeed analysis revealed it to be a net-net, with a solid margin of safety despite the very high levels of debt. By the time Peter had completed his position at an average price of $1.63 it was by some margin the fund's largest position.

The price, nevertheless, continued its precipitous decline to well under a dollar and the gossip on the street was bankruptcy – not something that would normally have fazed Peter. But there was another factor. Brian McDermott was in charge of marketing the Value Fund and he regarded Westar as a position that stood out like a sore thumb as an example of persistent folly and believed that it was responsible for deterring many investment advisors, particularly in British Columbia, from recommending that their clients buy the Value Fund or stick with it. Peter caved in, selling out the majority of the position at under 50 cents. A few months later the shares had rebounded to well over $2.00.

13

Per Ardua ad Astra

THE EARLY 1990S WERE BEDEVILLED by a succession of disappointing investments, not just LTV, and 1990 itself had been the first loss-making year in the sixteen-year history of the Value Fund – down 9%. Even more unsettling for Peter were two further years of pedestrian results: plus 5% in 1991 and plus 7% in 1992, which prompted him to confide to his journal:

> I am off balance at the moment – not in harmony. The problem is partly professional. I feel sort of stuck – no triumphs, only little glimpses of light, which have so far kept me on a level, as it were compensating for the mistakes. I am working just as hard as ever, but seemingly not so productively. I think I may be preparing for a fierce challenge."

And indeed it was not long in coming. By early July he was writing:

> Professionally everything is going wrong; the Canadian dollar is strong, not weak as I expected. The Fed has become concerned about the strains on the credit system and so it's lowering interest rates. A strong stock market is the result. LTV looks as though it will take much longer to resolve than I anticipated.

The recession, if this is what it is, has barely begun and the market has assumed that it will soon be over anyway. The "looking over the valley" syndrome is in fashion. Do we have too much cash!?

He set off for a Cundill International Company board meeting in Bermuda in a slightly better frame of mind because the Japanese market was still falling, growth stocks had been suffering, the financial press were making a story of "gloom and doom," and it seemed possible that his caution might yet be vindicated.

I realized that my competitors got killed this week – we didn't – we have the treasure trove of over two hundred million dollars in cash.

As markets continued to decline Peter was, most unusually, torn by indecision:

I find myself thinking about buying things with $250 million of cash reserves and a good many net-nets about, although world events, plus the economic uncertainties could in reality spell "crash." I am alert both to the danger and the opportunity and I can't decide which it is. I need to put my mind in park and think intuitively. No formula works forever, it needs to be in continuous review and development. I need to be receptive to new ideas and not just to dismiss them out of hand. Keep looking for the spark. Think about how you communicate – how to set about sparking off other people and how to make it easier for them to spark off you.

I think I should be optimistic. There are plenty of statistical bargains available in the world. Everyone else is now depressed and highly pessimistic. Ought I to continue to be cautious – it isn't what the numbers are now telling me, but I'm finding it hard at the moment to ignore the sentiment around me. Sometimes a flippant remark allows the spikes of reason to penetrate the brain. I should be reading plenty of poetry, if for no other reason than that it appeals directly to the intuitive side of the brain.

Christmas celebrated at the Canyon Ranch resort in Arizona provided a moment of catharsis. There was the routine of Christmas Eve, work and family phone calls in the day, and then chicken in puff pastry, the recitation of the annual "grace," and Peter's "state of the family finances" speech in which he articulated his fears and his hopes, after which he felt a certain release and fell quietly to sleep in front of the fire, before creeping off to bed. He was the first up in the morning and was able to read beside the Christmas tree for a couple of hours, sipping coffee and imbibing the peace of the sleeping house. But the mood had not entirely lifted and the next night he woke in the early hours in a cold sweat, worrying about the business and his ability as an investment manager.

He wrote down two significant quotations in his journal. The first is from Nietzsche's *Beyond Good and Evil:*

> Gaze not too long into the abyss, lest the abyss gaze back at you.

It is followed by the opening lines from Dante's *Inferno.*

> In the midst of the path of my life
> I found myself in a dark wood,
> In which the right path was obscured.

> I cannot express how hard it was
> To find myself in this untamed forest,
> So bitter and so tenacious was it
> That the mere thought of it renews my terrors.

By the middle of February 1992 the spectres of doubt had been laid to rest and he was composing the letter to "fellow investors" that was routinely attached to the annual report of the Cundill Value Fund. He began in typically uncompromising fashion:

> 1991 was undistinguished. However, it was an important year of transition. Two significant factors were at play.
>
> - The portfolio has been concentrated. The number of holdings has been decreased by approximately one-third and the average size of position increased by 20%. Our focus, but especially my own, has consequently been considerably sharpened. My father was a very good birdshot and he always said "never shoot into the brown." In other words, never shoot into a flock of birds without first choosing a single bird – at least in your mind.
> - We continue to be "value orientated." The equity components of the Cundill Value Fund as at December 31st traded at approximately 64% of book value. By comparison and also at year end, the securities that comprise the Standard and Poor's 500 traded at 270% of book value and the TSE 300 at 130% of book value. If our shares were to trade at the same book value as these two indices instead of at a fraction of book value, the increase to our investors' rate of return would be significant. But discounts to asset value are not enough, in the long run you need earnings to be able to sustain and nurture these corporate values. We now, as a matter of

course, ask ourselves hard questions as to where we expect each business to be in the future and, as well, make a judgement on the quality of the management.

He also commented on Japan:

Japan is going through a period of significant adjustment. From March 1987 until the beginning of 1991 we were short Japan. [Peter had bought put options on the Japanese Nikkei 500 index.] This was not a hedging strategy, nor was it a contradiction in terms of our basic Benjamin Graham value principles. It was a development thereon to which I attribute the term the "antithesis of value." What I mean by this is identifying a market where values are so stretched and extreme that they are clearly unsustainable. They have passed far beyond the realms of any measure of statistical common sense. I believed that to be the case with Japan. It was tough and it took endurance but in the end it was very right. Now, however, we are beginning to find opportunities in Japan, not on an earnings basis, but on a balance sheet basis, where selected Japanese companies' shares are trading at a discount to liquidation value.

But it was not until 1993 that the restructuring of the portfolio and the adjusted strategy really paid off. As markets began to turn in his favour at the beginning of the year Peter's enthusiasm is self evident, but so are the scars or, as he would probably have preferred to express it, the bruises of some lessons learnt in the field of battle:

Stock markets are in full bloom and a lot of our stuff is moving, albeit on thin volume. I am reviewing numbers and accounts daily as heretofore. From now on I shall not be influenced by others making depressive assumptions which, when taken on board, sometimes exhibit a tendency to be self fulfilling. By the same token I am determined to endeavour to ignore my own hopes and expectations, converting them to no particular hopes or expectations – just a determination to do an exceptional job. On that note I had a glass of champagne and a cigar and then went to bed and slept like a baby.

By the end of the year – its nineteenth – the Value Fund was up 43% for a compound return since inception of 19%. The doubters melted away and it was to Peter's special satisfaction that the European investments that he had pioneered and which now represented over a quarter of the total portfolio had made an exceptional contribution, almost doubling in value. He had also dipped his toe into the water on the buy side again in Japan.

One of the European success stories of that period was The Telegraph plc, which published one of Britain's oldest and most respected daily broadsheets, and it is a further example of the way in which Peter was prepared creatively to adapt the Ben Graham value framework when he felt that the margin of safety justified it. The paper was controlled by a number of family trusts related to the founding Berry family, but by then the family had proliferated and they were now somewhat lukewarm shareholders. Peter noticed that Conrad Black was beginning to accumulate a shareholding; he had known Conrad nearly all his life and had considerable respect for his business acumen, especially in anything related to publishing, so he was prompted to have a look at the Telegraph business.

At first glance it did not appear to be strictly a net-net but there was a considerable asset cushion and it was winning its price war with Murdoch's *London Times* and had a far larger circulation. But the real key, as Peter saw it, was that it had a 25% stake in John Fairfax Holdings, an Australian newspaper chain. The shares were trading at just over £4.00 per share.

Peter's analysis was that News Corporation (Murdoch) was stretched because it was loaded with debt and therefore precariously placed to absorb the rising costs of newsprint, leaving the *Telegraph* in the dominant position with respect to pricing, and with Conrad running the show it would be very well administered. The icing on the cake was that the book value of the Fairfax holding plus its 10% of Southam amounted to £2.21 per Telegraph share so that one was buying the newspaper itself for less than £2.00 per share. Peter summed it up:

> If you apply American newspaper measures, the real value of the paper ought to be at least twice the value that it's currently priced at in the market and if you assume that Fairfax could be sold at a premium to book, which I think highly probable, it's a steal because you can fairly argue that you're actually paying almost zero for the newspaper company.

Peter accumulated a position in the company that made it the largest single holding in the Value Fund (7%) at the time and he paid several calls on The Telegraph, meeting both with Conrad and Danny Coulson, the CEO and deputy chair. They were always cordial meetings and Peter was given the impression that his support was appreciated and that in due course he would be "looked after," although given the margin of safety he had no real concerns on that score. He did, nevertheless, express his views about the discrepancy between US valuations of newspaper publishing assets and those pertaining in the UK and Canada and this may well have influenced Conrad in his decision to list Hollinger, the holding company for his publishing assets, in the United States – a move that enabled him to raise a significant tranche of equity there but which also exposed him to the US regulatory authorities that proved to be his nemesis. By then the Value Fund had long since been bought out at a handsome profit.

At about the same time Peter began to buy another newspaper company, this time in Switzerland, and it was to illustrate for him some of the arcane workings of European stock market regulation. Neue Zürcher Zeitung was the holding company for Switzerland's leading financial newspaper with circulation throughout Switzerland and much of Germany, as Peter described it:

> "It's a serious newspaper. A bit like *Barron's* and with even fewer photographs, but full of gnomic wisdom.

The shares were extremely illiquid and were subject to some draconian voting restrictions, limiting the voting to members of specific political parties and residents of particular Swiss cantons. It was, however, a classic net-net, trading at under 60% of book value. A thorough examination of the assets went much further – NZZ had a stack of assets that showed it to be selling at less than 30% of its conservative liquidation value – a huge margin of safety – in addition to which it had no debt and a virtually unassailable franchise. There was not a shadow of doubt that the value was there; the issue, of course, was time – how long would it be before it was recognized?

Patience being Peter's watchword this did not concern him unduly, but he did have a hunch that the winds of change, in terms of corporate governance and concern for minority shareholders' rights, were beginning to waft across Europe and that even Zurich, the ultimate bastion of conservatism, might not be immune. His expectations were not fulfilled in quite the way he had anticipated but the sense that there might be a Pandora's box threatening to open had percolated far enough that the Zurich establishment in the Bahnhofstrasse were extremely wary of anything that might just loosen the lid.

With a holding of 6% of NZZ the Value Fund had become the company's single largest shareholder but it was having great difficulty in registering the shares and the fund's custodian bank was becoming anxious about this because the responses to its requests were becoming increasingly evasive. Peter was enjoying his annual walking break in the mountains above Interlaken and on his way back to London he stopped off in Zurich. He called on NZZ's finance director. He was cordially but cautiously received. It was clear the management were unsure about his intentions and uncomfortable with the fund's shareholding. Peter gave his candid assessment of the underlying values and then broached the problems being encountered over the share registration. Ten minutes later he was strolling back to the Hotel Baur au Lac having shaken hands on a deal to sell the fund's block of stock back to the company at a substantial profit.

One of the essential traits of the successful "vulture" value investor is instinct. One needs not just to smell the lion's carcass from afar but to be able to imagine that the bees may have made honey inside it. Peter had been eyeing the French market for some time. He believed that the corporate culture was changing – the pendulum beginning to swing in favour of realizing value for the ordinary shareholder – but his intuition had been to await some event that might turn French stock market bargains into outright steals. In mid 1995 Paris erupted into an orgy of riot and destruction and Peter's attention was immediately focused. Investors were rushing for the exit, dumping French stocks without regard for long term perspective. As Peter put it later:

> People in France were throwing fire bombs, there was a general strike, and live pictures of all this were to be viewed on every television news channel and that is often a good time to buy securities.

He already had a history of success with finding value in oversold or neglected financial companies – Credit Foncier Franco Canadien was his first significant investment success – and so he turned his attention to one of the largest in France – Paribas, coincidentally the parent of CFFC. As a result he was already pretty familiar with the institution and he began to accumulate a position. Not unusually, even after the debacle caused by the rioting, he was too early, but his analysis, representing the case to the board of the Value Fund for significantly adding to the position, makes interesting reading:

> Paribas was founded in 1872 as a bank that specialized in the creation of new investment opportunities for their own account and for clients. They were a wholesale deposit gatherer and a lending bank (not retail) as well. By 1981, they were the paramount *banque d'affaires* in France. And then they were nationalized by the new Socialist government. This did their business no favours and in 1986 the bank was privatized again, although there was a *noyau dur* or hard-core shareholder group who remained sympathetic to the government of the day.
>
> The easiest way to think of Paribas is as a holding company with four separate subsidiary operations:
> - Banque Paribas – the original bank doing money management, derivative trading, investment banking, etc.
> - Compagnie Bancaire – a specialized financial company with subsidiaries focused on leasing and consumer finance. It is 47% owned and has its own market quotation.
> - Credit du Nord – a retail bank.
> - Paribas Affaires Industrielles that manages a portfolio of equity holdings which at December 31st 1995 amounted to some $8.4 billion. These investments cross corporate lines!

The recent earnings history is as follows: a loss in 1991, modest earnings increases through to 1994, and then a whopping loss in 1995, much of which, *nota bene*, was provisioning. It would appear that there are very few possible bad surprises left in the cupboard. But, this is a banking group!

As to recent price movements, the high was 528ff in 1994 and the low 249ff in 1995. Today's price (July 1996) is 295ff.

In early 1996, the holding company purchased the remaining 57% that it did not own of Navigation Mixte. This company, inter alia, owned 8.6% of Paribas itself. The effective number of Paribas shares outstanding has thereby been reduced to 106 million shares and in fact they bought in those shares at below book value. The negative goodwill has been used to reduce the carrying value of the investments. Much of the investment portfolio has been sold at highly satisfactory numbers, reducing the debt of the holding company. The capital gains realized in this operation and other sales have resulted in capital gains of some $4 billion francs that will be counted as an ongoing profit and loss item in 1996. Since there are significant tax loss carry-forwards, these will be tax free transactions.

The earnings estimates for the year range between 3 billion and 6 billion francs. If you will forgive the rough arithmetic, using 100 million shares outstanding this is between 30 and 60 francs per share. Much of this is in the bag already.

As to Net Asset Value estimates, our preferred benchmark of value, the range is between 490 and 553 francs depending on how tough you are on the capital gains tax. There is additional value in Credit du Nord and it is openly up for sale.

The positives on this investment are as follows:

- Earnings this year will be good.

- There is a solid margin of safety in the NAV.
- Management is trying to simplify the range of activities and to focus on what they do best.
- There is no majority shareholder. This is a takeover or merger candidate.

The negatives are as follows:

- There have been a series of fiefdoms; it will be difficult to change the culture. It is difficult and costly to reduce head count in France.
- There could be more bad surprises in the real estate or the trading areas.
- The French share market could collapse.
- There is debt at the holding company level.

My conviction is that at the current level of 300 francs there is a decent margin of safety to overcome potential problems. The operating environment is satisfactory with low interest rates. There is always the possibility of a deal. These shares are to be purchased aggressively.

And buy them he did. By the end of the year it was by some margin the Value Fund's largest holding. There were several other French holdings, making it, at 17%, the single largest market in which the fund was invested.

14

The Perfect Match

ONE FEATURE THAT APPEARS to be common to most of the great investors is that they are proselytizers, exhibiting a general willingness to mentor and instruct "disciples." Peter is no exception. He is such an enthusiast for his profession, and especially for his own particular corner of it – value investment within a Ben Graham framework, shaped along Cundill lines – that he has always been eager to share his knowledge even, in a sense, to evangelize. The results of this were not only "Pete's Mornings" at the annual Cundill conference but a steady stream of speaking engagements at business schools, investment seminars, and the like, at which he would not only expound theory but was fully prepared to share the details of his real experience, both the good and the bad.

In the context of his own fund management business this openness and willingness to talk about the investment process to all and sundry, provided that they evinced a genuine interest, resulted in an eclectic and creative group of employees within Cundill Investment Research Limited.

This entity had been set up in the early 1990s to support Peter in the analytical process and it evolved over the years into an organization that encouraged lively debate based on solidly grounded research work. In due course several members of the team attained the status of portfolio manager, in particular Tim McElvaine, who now runs his own fund management company, and Andy Massie, who remains with Mackenzie Cundill and manages the Mackenzie Cundill Value Fund. However, Peter's attitude to any form of "collegiate" decision making was made very clear in an article in the *Outstanding Investor's Digest* in 1988:

> To my knowledge there are no good records that have been built by institutions run by committee. In almost all cases the great records are the product of individuals, perhaps working together, but always within a clearly defined framework. Their names are on the door and they are quite visible to the investing public. In reality outstanding records are made by dictators, hopefully benevolent, but nonetheless dictators. And another thing, most top managers really do exchange ideas without fear or ego. They always will. I don't think I've ever walked into an excellent investor's office who hasn't openly said "Yeah sure, here's what I'm doing." or, "What did you do about that one? I blew it." We all know we aren't always going to get it right and it's an invaluable thing to be able to talk to others who understand.

And it was true until Peter retired that he always remained the final arbiter, the ultimate decision maker in all portfolio matters, and it is still the case within the Mackenzie Cundill group of funds that there is in every fund either a single responsible fund manager or a *primus inter pares*. You know exactly who to pat on the back or the opposite.

But, of course, as yet the marriage with Mackenzie Financial Corporation (Mackenzie) had not taken place. As the 1990s progressed it was becoming increasingly apparent that in the mutual fund business small and specialist was fine – low fixed costs and no requirement for a substantial marketing budget – medium-sized, which was where Peter Cundill and Associates was then positioned, was problematic.

The fixed costs for a medium-sized fund management company are not so very different from those for a very substantial-sized one and, in order to promote growth of any consequence, the proportion of revenues that needs to be appropriated to marketing rises exponentially. On top of that, by the 1990s there had been some adjustments in fee structures; most importantly, the majority of "load" funds were by then offering a Deferred Sales Charge option, which Cundill could not afford to do, and this was becoming a serious impediment to sales. Shrinking or standing still are not attractive options and are generally disastrous for the energy and dynamics of a business, but increasing marketing budgets inevitably puts a squeeze on the bottom line, at least in the short term.

During 1994 Peter was interviewed by James Morton for a book that he was editing for London's *Financial Times*; *The Financial Times Global Guide to Investing – The Secrets of the World's Leading Investment Gurus*. The chapter in which Peter was included was called "Learning from Living Legends," Peter's own nomenclature being "The Patient Purist."

The two men had an immediate meeting of the minds. James, a graduate of Cambridge with an MBA and an MA in World Economics from Stanford, has an incisive mind. He was already an experienced money manager in international equities and thoroughly familiar with Graham and Dodd theory. Peter and he met on several occasions over the next few months and Peter quickly came to the conclusion that he wanted to somehow co-opt James into the Cundill team. A deal was struck the following year and James has, in the course of time, developed into the highly successful fund manager of the Mackenzie Cundill Recovery Fund and the Cundill International Company, two of the Mackenzie Cundill stable of funds.

At an earlier stage in his career James had worked for Bain and Co., the management consultants, and, as he and Peter became closer, Peter confided some of his concerns about the future of the business, profitable though it was. James was quick to see the crux of the problem and rapidly persuaded Peter that the only way to secure the future, without taking an enormous personal investment risk in ramping up the marketing expenses, was to sell to, or merge with, a much larger group with plenty of its own distribution and marketing muscle. The decision in principle was taken immediately, but finding the right bridegroom was not so straightforward.

However, as had happened so often in Peter's career, lady luck intervened, this time in the shape of Mackenzie. Mackenzie was the second largest fund company in Canada. It sold its products through independent brokers and dealers and offered an extensive range of vehicles, more than fifty separate fund choices, with just over $25 billion in assets and a sizeable and dedicated sales force that has access to 25,000 investment professionals across Canada. Peter, by comparison, was forty-first in the pecking order with less than half a billion in assets. But James Hunter, Mackenzie's CEO, and David Feather, head of product management, had noticed that their unitholders were becoming ever more hungry for product diversification and they had no classic "value" manager in their portfolio to provide them with this category of investment opportunity. Peter, with his enviable long-term record, was the obvious choice and, equally important, he was keen to do a deal.

What emerged in 1998, after some lengthy negotiations in which Peter had been careful not to appear overly eager, was what both parties referred to as a "strategic alliance." As Phil Cunningham, the president of Mackenzie Financial Services expressed it:

> This is one of those rare situations where you add one and get three. The alliance follows Mackenzie's philosophy of building a business by creating a haven for "good people."

From Peter's standpoint the arrangement was as near ideal as he could have hoped. Mackenzie assumed all of the marketing and administration responsibility and gave him a fifteen-year contract to manage what were now the Mackenzie Cundill Funds on terms that did not interfere in any way with his distinctive contrarian, value-based approach to investment. As well, no redundancies were necessary among the Cundill staff. The Deferred Sales Charge option was to be introduced immediately and it remained to be seen what the impact of 25,000 investment advisors operating within an exceptionally efficient marketing machine might be. Peter's instinct was that, as long as the performance was there, the result was likely to be a significant increase in the funds under his management – quite how much turned out to be beyond his wildest imaginings.

15

Entering the Big League

THE PERFORMANCE OF THE VALUE FUND in the years immediately following the stellar 43% gain of 1993 had been more pedestrian, although perfectly respectable, notching up a further 34.4% between 1994 and 1996. But Peter had made a major strategic switch out of Europe, especially the French market, into Japan and, as is so often the case with value investment, he was out too early and in too early.

It was not that European markets were statistically particularly overvalued. They were not. The crux of the matter was that many Japanese securities were beginning to be almost as cheap again in value terms as when John Templeton had "discovered" Japan in the early 1960s.

In a sense this was not surprising, given that the Nikkei 225 had dropped from its dizzy high of 40,000 in December 1990, when Peter was suffering maximum pain and gritting his teeth over his short position, to around 18,000 by December 1997. By then Peter was licking his lips in a predatory fashion and he needed to create the extra liquidity within the Value Fund to take advantage. As he himself put it in a lecture he gave some years later:

> We dined out in Europe, we had the biggest positions in Deutsche Bank and Paribas, which both had big investment

> portfolios, so you got the bank itself for nothing. You had a huge margin of safety – it was easy money. We had doubles and triples in those markets and we thought we were pretty smart, so in 1996 and 1997 we took our profits and took flight to Japan, which was just so beaten up and full of values. But in doing so we missed out on some five baggers, which is when the initial investment has multiplied five times, and we had to wait at least two years before Japan started to come good for us.
>
> This is a recurring problem for most value investors – that tendency to buy and to sell too early. The virtues of patience are severely tested and you get to thinking it's never going to work and then finally your ship comes home and you're so relieved that you sell before it's time. What we ought to do is go off to Bali or some such place and sit in the sun to avoid the temptation to sell too early.

In fact, by the end of 1997 the Value Fund was over 40% invested in Japan, but that country's bear market still had a sting in its tail. In the second half of 1998 the Nikkei dropped a further 4,000, down to 14,000. This was the first year of the new Mackenzie relationship and ironically it produced the second loss in the twenty-two-year history of the Value Fund – down 9% and underperforming the benchmarks. Much to the credit of the Mackenzie management team there were, despite this, no doubters as to the wisdom of the deal with Peter.

In point of fact Peter's seemingly precipitate move into Japan was not predicated simply on the numbers. He had long since learned that, while it is the numbers that provide the ultimate margin of safety, without some form of catalyst markets can ignore value for frustratingly long periods of time. As he explained it in a memorandum, the thing that had changed his stance from that of quietly nibbling away at a few cheap Japanese stocks toward making an aggressive shift of a major portion of the assets under his management into Japan was what he perceived to be a fundamental change in policy within Japan's bureaucracy:

> Japan has a big problem – a very extreme demographic problem. By the year 2025, 42% of Japanese will be retired. And although a similar pattern is true to a certain extent in all developed nations, it is a much greater problem in Japan because a much higher percentage of its population will be affected than that of any other nation. I recently visited with a very senior economist at one of the major Japanese banks who serves on a committee which advises the Japanese Ministry of Health, which in turn manages the Japanese pension fund – about $1 trillion.
>
> What she said was that there are three possible policy alternatives. They could tax the young more – but they are already approaching tax levels that would be economically damaging except in the very short term. They could reduce benefits to the elderly but that, apart from being socially unpalatable, is also very awkward politically because these people have votes and use them. But there is a much more acceptable alternative. As of now, Japanese pension funds are predominantly invested in Japanese government bonds carrying an interest rate of less than 2%. So the third alternative is to get their rate of return up. And, in fact, the whole thrust of the initiatives I see happening today is designed to achieve exactly that. The policy moves are based on the premise that Japan *has* to get its investment returns up. The initiatives for change are coming directly out of the Ministry of Finance and the Ministry for Overseas Trade.
>
> So what have they got to work with? First of all – and this is really quite key – every Japanese company owns pieces of other

companies – these are holdings which are first and foremost about relationships. If you like they are certificates of relationship – as distinct from certificates of value. Japanese companies would buy stakes in their suppliers, their bankers, and their customers because the purchase of those stakes was seen as part of the price of admission to doing business. In practice these holdings are just extra assets and they are not, as it were, inviolate. It has always been the case that companies could sell these holdings if they needed to, even if only to other companies. But the mood now is to encourage the development of shareholder value, if necessary by shaking up corporate governance and encouraging the sale of some of these historic holdings into the public arena.

This new mood is not just a chimera – since the beginning of 1997 Japanese companies have been allowed to buy back their own shares. In the last few months about 75 buybacks were not only announced but actually done for the first time ever in Japan. They have also introduced share options and what interests me about that is that each company that issues stock options is required to buy in sufficient of its own stock to cover the options. At major companies, managements are talking about increasing the returns on shareholders' equity.

Not so long ago I noted in my journal a comment from a senior executive at the Industrial Bank of Japan with whom I had raised the issue of shareholders' rights and corporate governance. He responded quite emphatically – "I don't know what you're talking about. In a Japanese company, first and foremost comes the employee, then the customer. Thirdly come the bank and the suppliers. Here at the bank we own 4–5% of every publicly listed Japanese company and in my twenty years here I never heard the concept of shareholders' rights discussed, not ever!" This is no longer the case.

THERE'S LOTS TO LIKE ABOUT JAPANESE STOCKS – PRICES, BALANCE SHEETS, & CASH FLOW.

Relative to earnings Japan is still expensive. But ASSETS......!

However, because this is such an important strategic move for us I want to move from the general to the particular. One of the Ben Graham tests was to buy securities at their lows – ideally close to their all-time lows, but certainly close to their five-year lows. In Japan today there are many securities that meet that test. I want to explore a case study but you must bear in mind that it is far from unique. Tokyo Style mainly manufactures and sells women's clothing; it hit a five-year low of Y1,150 in early 1997 – down from an all-time high of just over Y3,000. It has cash and securities totalling Y138 billion which equates to Y1,367 per share – more than the current share price – and it has negligible long term debt – a mere Y166 million – less than Y2 per share. You would be hard pressed to find anything similar in Europe or North America even if you went back as far as the 1973/5 bear market.

But we do not just look at the balance sheet; in addition we look at cash-flow. Like many other companies in Japan Tokyo Style is generating lots of cash – Y5.5 billion of it – and its capital expenditure is less than 10% of this, so the majority is disposable cash-flow. We have also conducted an exercise looking at earnings using GAAP. To return to the case study, Tokyo Style's return on equity is low – only 2.6% – but this is typical of nearly all Japanese companies. They have very low returns on equity partly because they take lots of depreciation. Adjusting their depreciation to US levels would push it up to about

4% – still pretty low. But across the board if you adjust the P/E ratios to US GAAP they are not actually that high and many are selling at 8 or 9 times cash-flow and while dividend yields do not seem high, surprisingly enough they are higher than many US Corporations.

I have always felt that cash was a terrific thing to have but Japanese companies earn less than 1% on their deposits and in some cases zero. The last time that you could get a dividend yield in the US in excess of the short term cost of money was in the late 40s and early 50s. So I have no misgivings about our major switch into Japan.

By this time Peter could fairly be considered an old hand at Japan. He had made his first visit to the country in 1969 and bought his first, and very successful, investments there in 1985, during the brief shakeout that happened prior to the Nikkei rising virtually without pause from 10,000 to 40,000 by 1990. One of these investments was Matsushita Electric, perhaps better known outside Japan by its brand names of JVC and Panasonic. He had bought the shares below book and liquidation value and sold them again in 1987 when they reached three times book value. He had bought them again steadily through 1989, 1990, and 1991 because they had again sunk below book value. He had done this at the very same time that he was shorting the overvalued Japanese index – so that he was buying more Matsushita at exactly the same time he was so painfully rolling over the Nikkei put options – the point being that, as always, his individual investment decisions were predominantly value driven and determined by the numbers. The fact that overall the Japanese market at the time was so grossly overvalued that he was shorting it mattered not a jot, as long as he could clearly see that essential margin of safety in a particular security. And the love affair continued: by 1995 Matsushita was again selling at a discount to liquidation value. He bought it again and bought more as the Nikkei fell through 1997 and 1998, finally buying the last of the position in January 1999.

Peter's call on Japan may have been early but it was absolutely correct. In 1999 the previous year's setback in the Value Fund was more than reversed with a 16% gain, followed by a further 20% in 2000. With nearly 50% invested in Japan, it was the prime contributor to these results. It had been a classic contrarian call, adding considerably to Peter's reputation. Individually the investments were across a range of sectors from financials to pharmaceutical, the only common feature being that they had all been trading below liquidation value. Like all classic value investors, Peter had no concern whatsoever with what business a company was engaged just as long as it met the financial criteria.

A good illustration of this point was Tokyo Broadcasting System. It was the third largest television broadcaster in Japan and, along with its competitors, had suffered a sharp decline in its advertising revenues as the Japanese economy had stagnated through the 1990s. On the face of it, it was not very appealing except as a recovery situation, but there were plenty of those around that would in all probability reap more immediate rewards than TBS if the macro-economic situation in Japan improved. The TBS management was competent rather than imaginative or creative. Most investors would not have given it a second glance. Not so Peter. Someone had remarked that TBS might be cheap so he took a quick look and then a more careful one. He discovered that TBS owned valuable property and had lots of cash as well as an investment portfolio.

These were the sums:

Share price	Y1,500
Value of real estate per share	Y1,000
Cash and share portfolio per share	Y500

There was the margin of safety. At that share price you were buying the business for nothing and Peter valued this, on liquidation principles, at Y2,000, which gave him a "fair value" of Y3,500. He began buying in 1998 and accumulated the majority of his position through 2001 and 2002 at prices below Y1500. Most of it was sold at between Y2,500 and Y3,000, although the shares did in fact eventually reach Peter's "fair value" of Y3,500.

There were, logically enough, some very positive side effects resulting from Peter's latest success with Japan. In the fall of 1998 Mackenzie launched a new product: its Universal Select Managers Fund. The fund was to have an international focus and was to be invested by five separate fund managers with widely different strategies. Peter was to be one of these managers, which was a brave choice by Mackenzie at that date.

Initially Peter's share was a mere $200,000 but, as his returns began to be recognized by the Mackenzie sales force and the investing public, purchases of the Select Fund as well as the Value Fund began to gather momentum. Within the Select Fund new money was allocated according to the relative performance of the various managers and when the growth stock boom collapsed in 2000 both Peter's absolute and relative performance were seen to be outstanding. By March 2001 his share of the Select Fund was about $1.5 billion. As Peter noted in a memorandum to his team at the time, the Mackenzie relationship had turned into a "win win" situation.

He went on to make some interesting more personal comments:

> I am thinking about where I should like to go in my passage through life. This business has been very good to me. It has allowed me an extraordinary amount of freedom on many levels. In some ways the Cundill brand is established and getting to the point where it will not need the founder's presence to prosper. I

don't think it's quite there yet but if collectively we continue to work together, we can achieve the goal of long term continuity, nurturing the team we have built and the value based backbone of our investment philosophy, through which we have been able over the years to provide above average returns to our loyal investors. I have also reflected that I am myself one of those investors in that I now have about $75 million of my own money invested in Cundill products. I am not the largest client but I have a very direct stake in our ongoing success.

This is still the case.

16

There's Always Something Left to Learn

THE EARLY YEARS of the new millennium were generally favourable for the value investor. It was never easy but, quite often during that period, it turned out that less patience than usual was required for a value investment to be recognized by the market. Nevertheless, pitfalls always abounded. Peter has an enviable gift for avoiding the majority of them and this is not just based on doing the numbers and adhering rigorously to the Ben Graham framework. It springs from an instinct resulting from years of experience – a nose for when, even though a set of accounts may have all the appearance of perfect rectitude, there is something that does not give off comfortable vibrations.

An excellent example of this is the tale of Brascan, in which he invested heavily, building up close to a 5% stake, and Nortel, in which he did not. Brascan was and still is (in its new guise as Brookfield Asset Management) a Toronto-based conglomerate made up of real-estate, financial services, and power generation. Nortel was a high technology telecommunications company with a multi-billion-dollar market capitalization – the darling of the majority of the investment community. It no longer exists, having gone spectacularly bankrupt some years ago, leaving zero value for its stockholders. By contrast Brascan was viewed as very dull, if not actually risky.

In the latter part of 1999 Peter was giving a presentation to a large group of investment representatives and faced some quite aggressive questioning from the floor as to what he was doing with a substantial holding in a boring old stock like Brascan when he could be putting the money to better use in a high flier like Nortel – this, of course, was some time before the high technology crash. Never one to duck a challenge, Peter decided to run a comparison of the two companies, which he presented at the Cundill Conference in 2000.

As is clear from the table, Brascan at $18.00 was still trading at a small discount to its book value of $19.10. At $73, with a book value of $6.25, Nortel, equally obviously, was not. All of the comparative statistics are revealing, but one might focus on just two others that ought to have given the Nortel advocates pause. Brascan's P/E ratio was 12.4, Nortel's was 97, and Brascan had a dividend yield of 5.1% versus 0.10% for Nortel. The table was accompanied by a note from Peter to his investment team in Vancouver:

> As you know I called for a brief comparison between Brascan and Nortel. Brascan is cheap; Nortel is dear. We all know that. I have spent time trying to understand the latter. When I was studying for my CFA in 1968, it was the heyday of the "concept stock," the conglomerate based on the pooling-of-interest accounting, lofty multiples, and inspiring dreams. The backdrop was the Vietnam War: Treasury Bills in the US were slightly over five per cent and inflation was around the same number. Abraham Brilloff was writing articles on "Unaccountable Accounting" and "Dirty Pooling." Nobody cared; accounting is a bear market phenomenon! On the face of it Nortel is not *that* bad. It seems to be writing off at least some purchased goodwill [Nortel had made a lot of high-priced acquisitions in the previous few years] through the Profit and Loss account, paving the

Comparative statistics for Brascan and Nortel sent by Peter from Hong Kong to his investment team in Vancouver.

July 18, 2000

Good Morning:
CIR – I am attaching the brief statistical review of Brascan and Nortel. In addition, I am attaching the audited P&L statement for Nortel in the prior two years. On the face of it Nortel lost money in the last two years! Am I correct? Or am I just being a curmudgeon who knows nothing about anything?

Brascan vs. Nortel		1995	1996	1997	1998	1999
Price Dec 31 (CDN)	Brascan	$13.88	$20.60	$26.00	$21.30	$19.10
	Nortel	$7.30	$10.65	$15.89	$19.15	$72.93
Book value/per share	Brascan	$17.43	$17.47	$20.01	$20.58	$21.72
	Nortel	$2.55	$2.97	$3.30	$6.35	$6.25
EPS	Brascan	$1.57	$1.28	$3.34	$2.12	$2.15
	Brascan (before gains)	$1.20	$1.28	$1.39	$1.00	$1.53
	Nortel	$0.60	$0.40	$0.50	$0.70	$0.80
P/E ratio	Brascan	11.6	16.1	18.7	21.3	12.4
	Nortel	11.6	26.0	34.6	29.4	97.0
Return on Equity	Brascan	7.5%	6.1%	15.1%	10.7%	10.4%
	Nortel	24.6%	13.8%	13.9%	10.3%	12.03%
Dividend yield	Brascan	8.1%	4.8%	3.8%	4.8%	5.1%
	Nortel	0.72%	0.59%	0.46%	0.39%	0.1%

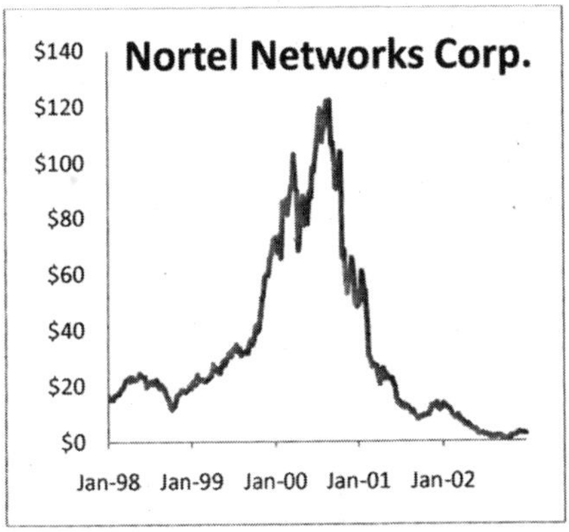

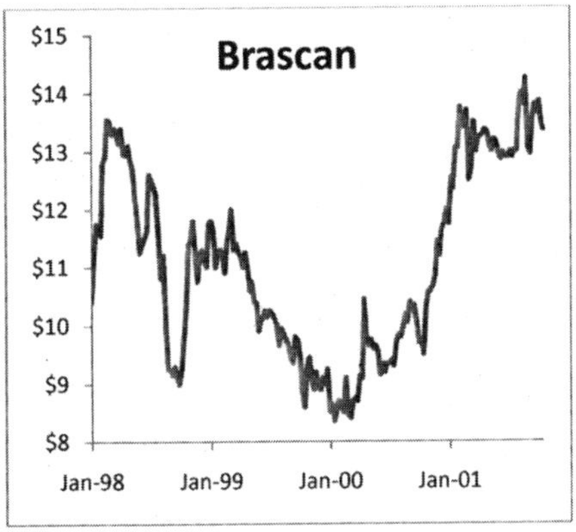

way for better Rates of Return on equity in the future. My own view is that the company has been making big and uncertain technology bets, while the marketplace is convinced that these will all work. Such chickens have a tendency to come home to roost. I would like to leave you with two insights in finding a good investment and to tell you the story of the 100th monkey. First the insights:

- Every company ought to have an escape valve: inventory that can readily be reduced, a division that can be sold, a marketable investment portfolio, an ability to shed staff quickly. That sort of thing. However, no escape valve will provide a cushion in the face of a collapse in investor confidence.
- The business must be getting better, not necessarily by a lot, just honestly better.

Now for the story:

"In the 1950s scientists were studying Japanese monkeys on the island of Koshima. They provided the monkeys with sweet potatoes dropped in the sand; the monkeys liked the sweet potatoes but hated the sand. Then a young female named Imo found she could solve the problem by washing the potatoes in a nearby stream. She taught this trick to her mother. Her playmates learnt it too and taught their mothers.

In the following years, all the young monkeys learned how to wash the potatoes and taught their parents. Those adults unable to learn from their children carried on eating dirty potatoes.

Then something startling took place. In the fall of 1958, a certain number of monkeys were washing potatoes – we don't know exactly how many. But let's suppose that as the sun rose that morning there were ninety-nine monkeys washing potatoes and let us then suppose that later the same morning, the hundredth monkey learned to wash potatoes.

That's when it happened.

By that evening the whole tribe of monkeys was washing the potatoes before they ate them. The additional energy of that hundredth monkey had somehow created an ideological breakthrough and everyone jumped on the band-wagon."

Now this tale may be mythical but its implications are not, as we shall no doubt learn, in due course, in respect of Brascan and Nortel and much else!

Peter never at any stage bought Nortel; he did make a significant amount of money out of Brascan and its satellites.

Surprisingly enough, however, the worst investment that Peter ever made was in the telecommunications business. Over the years he had made some very big gains in that industry, Telefonos de Mexico and Philippine Long Distance Telephone to name only two. But Cable & Wireless was another matter and even more surprising, if only because in its acquisition strategy and technological ambitions it bore some similarity to Nortel.

The company had a very long history. It had started life in the nineteenth century as the establisher of telegraphic connections across the British Empire, which had once straddled the planet and governed the lives of over a third of its population in fifty countries. Marconi had been a director of the company and, as the world moved from telegraph to telephone, C&W had laid the necessary cabling and in many cases ran the networks.

It had been a leading player in the rapidly growing and ever-evolving industry. However by the late 1990s the company had surrendered most of its networks as colony after colony had become independent and was largely confined to the Caribbean and as a secondary player in the deregulated British domestic market. It appeared tired and to have lost its way. There had been unseemly boardroom squabbles between the CEO and Lord Young, the executive chair – a "Thatcherite" ex-Tory minister who had been parachuted in. The shares had gradually drifted down from a high of £15.00 to about £6.00 by the end of 1998. In spite of C&W's popular acquisition of MCI Communication's internet backbone business, analysts took the view that the company's balance sheet was too stretched to exploit the opportunity.

At the beginning of the following year a new CEO, Graham Wallace, was appointed. Wallace was a finance man and quickly set about addressing the balance sheet problem with a series of well negotiated disposals at good prices; One2One, the mobile phone business, went to Deutsche Telecom for £3.75 billion and the Cable & Wireless Optus business was well sold to Singapore Telephone. The effect of the sales was to transform C&W's balance sheet from net debt of £4 billion to a net cash position of £2.6 billion.

By this stage C&W was coming up on the radar for value buyers, including Peter, for whom it now had a lot to recommend it: no debt, cash on the balance sheet, profitable established networks, and a concentrated degree of market scepticism driving share prices down across the entire sector. A thorough analysis revealed a net asset value of £4.92, calculated on the basis of a conservative estimate of the realizable value of the "sum of the parts." The margin of safety was cash and marketable securities of £3.25 billion. The concern was that the company was in a highly competitive business but, as Peter had so often said, "we always look for the margin of safety in the balance sheet and then worry about the business." He began buying in March 2000 at just over £4.00.

In October he gave an interview in which he touched on the subject of C&W:

> There are two distinct points of view on this one. You can perfectly well make the case that the management has demonstrated its competence, having made highly satisfactory strategic sales, but there is a sense that maybe they will waste resources, and there is investor pressure, which is being resisted by the company, to give a fair amount of the proceeds back to the shareholders. This is a company with $20 billion of market capitalization, really large. The old institutional investors have gotten pretty beaten up and feel disinclined to give the new management much leeway and there are the other investors like ourselves who have bought in recently at significantly lower levels. As a general comment, we have never invested in high tech companies but now we do find ourselves buying things like Cable & Wireless, which are so low that they are trading below the amount of cash on hand. So, even though some of them have what we call "burn rates," meaning that they are spending cash as they go along for investment, marketing, and so on, a number of them are very interesting, including Cable & Wireless.

A modest burn rate, supplementing the free cash flow from the mature, low growth businesses in order to fund a planned investment program to promote C&W's ambitions to become a global provider of voice and data services to the business community and thus transform top line growth, was one thing. What actually happened was quite another.

Until this point Graham Wallace had been generally regarded as a relatively safe pair of hands unlikely to be tempted into the kind of acquisition spree overseen by his predecessor. This view entirely failed to anticipate the corrosive effect that a relentless stream of investment bankers, management consultants, and brokers, all preaching the same message, might have, even on an individual with a fairly balanced commercial sense. The pitch was simple – the market for internet-based services was growing at three times the rate for fixed-line telephone communication and the only quick way to dominate that market was by acquisition. Establishing a highly visible presence fast was more important than the price one was required to pay to achieve this.

Wallace was persuaded and a series of acquisitions followed over the next two years, ostensibly to provide that essential critical mass. Without exception, C&W paid top dollar for businesses that were loss-making and hungry for additional investment. Inevitably this had a detrimental effect on C&W's bottom line. At the same time the market was experiencing a sharp slowdown in the demand for capacity (bandwidth) from other telecoms companies in response to a tightening of corporate IT budgets. The result was four separate profit warnings in eighteen months. At the time of the fourth one in September 2002 the last vestiges of investor confidence evaporated and the share price collapsed to just over £1.00, a level not seen for two decades.

Thus far Peter had stuck with it, perhaps recalling the unfortunate premature exit he had made from Westar years earlier and his stoical renewals of the Nikkei puts, and he had added to the position on the way down. Nevertheless, by this stage even he was becoming seriously worried – schooled though he was in the value buyer's principle of "patience, patience, and yet more patience." What he feared was that he might be witnessing the dissipation of the entire margin of safety.

Most troublesome of all was the fact that, for all the cash that had been thrown at them, there was no discernable indication that the "dream" businesses were improving. Reassurances from the company began to have the ring of desperation and Peter was beginning to be uncomfortable with the accounting. On 13 November the company shocked the market by announcing an emergency restructuring and a £4.4 billon loss. Peter had to contemplate a grim reality: there was now a significant risk that C&W would not survive. After a conference call from Kyoto with the investment team in Vancouver, Peter gave the order to sell the whole position in the Value Fund. It was a bitter pill. He had invested just under $100 million in C&W, roughly 6% of the fund. The loss was nearly $59 million and it was very largely responsible for the fund posting an 11% loss for 2002.

However, as events unfolded, it became apparent that he had actually sold in the nick of time. A week before Christmas news leaked out that the company had a potential tax liability of a further £1.5 billion. Within hours the shares had halved again. The full sorry picture emerged over the next few months. Around £5 billion had been spent on internet ventures, principally in the US, that were now practically worthless and thousands of jobs were axed from the global division. There had been inexcusably poor tracking of the cash position, late disclosure of a tax liability relating to the sale of One2One to Deutsche Telecom, and the discovery of an £800 million black hole, a sum that was required to cover property leases. The Association of British Insurers called for an investigation into the failure to disclose the tax liability in a timely fashion. The company never recovered, although it still totters along, a shadow of its former self.

While no doubt experiencing a sense of relief that his eleventh hour sale had avoided the final debacle, Peter penned a memo to the Cundill Investment Research Group on Christmas Eve:

> Over the holiday we should all muse as to why we screwed up so badly on Cable & Wireless. There was really no dissenting voice. We can debate the issue in the New Year.

The conclusions of that debate form part of a lecture that Peter gave three years later at the Benjamin Graham Value Centre:

> The worst investment we have ever had was Cable & Wireless, which had built up a large cash pile through the sale of telephone companies in Hong Kong and Australia and their mobile telephone business in the UK. They were well negotiated, judicious sales. What they had left was a stand-alone operation in the Caribbean, which still exists, and they were in the fibre optic business that was blowing cash. So we said, look they've got cash, they've got a valuable, viable business and let's assume the fibre optic business is worth zero – it wasn't, it was worth less than zero, much, much less! Their accounting was flawed to say the least and they became obsessed by a technological dream. In this respect it was reminiscent of Nortel and that should have caused me to think twice.
>
> I talked to John Templeton about it afterwards and he took a worse hit than us. He said "this is why we diversify, if you are right 60% of the time and wrong 40% you're always going to be a hero, if you are right 40% of the time and wrong 60% you will be a bum." I think he probably put it more elegantly than that! But there's one more thing. We had put a huge amount of time and energy into that one and we were willing it to save itself and, on the face of it, it could have. What we needed was a dissenter in the team – a contrarian among contrarians, a lateral thinker watching out for the left field. On that occasion there wasn't one. So my thought is, if there's no natural sceptic on an investment maybe it would be wise to appoint one of the team to play Devil's Advocate anyway.

17

Dancing with the Witch Doctor

DUE DILIGENCE CAN TAKE MANY FORMS and in Peter's case, in pursuit of thoroughness, it most certainly did. This particular investment tale begins in 2002. In the wake of 9/11 oil prices began to rise sharply, reflecting the increasing political uncertainty in the Middle East and the explosive growth being experienced in China. This rapidly turned into a hot market for oil stocks – one in which Peter was not participating since there were no net-net's amongst the oil companies.

Discipline in investment matters being his watchword, Peter was not listening to the arguments of some of his investment team who wanted to bend the value criteria and participate. Eventually, more to put an end to the grumbling than for any other reason, he let it be known that if anyone could find him an oil company that was trading below cash, he would buy it, no questions asked – or nearly.

The challenge, of course, was taken up but without much success until Peter's cousin Geoffrey Scott, who was consulting for Cundill Investment Research Ltd (CIR), ferreted out a neglected name: Pan Ocean Energy Corporation Ltd.

It was run by David Lyons, a Calgarian living in Vancouver, whose father, Vern Lyons, had founded Ocelot Energy. When David took over he had quickly reached the conclusion that there was little future for small to medium sized oil companies operating in the US and Canada. There was far too much competition and the risk/reward was comparatively unattractive. Apart from that, the Ocelot balance sheet was far too stretched for it to properly exploit some of the good North American properties in its portfolio. Involving one of the majors in the process would inevitably mean massive dilution. Lyons was far too smart for that.

What he did was to merge his own small Pan Ocean Energy with Ocelot and then sell off Ocelot's entire North American and other peripheral parts of the portfolio, clean up the balance sheet, and bank the cash. He then looked overseas and determined that he would concentrate on deals in Sub-Saharan Africa, where licences could be secured for a fraction of the price tag that would apply in his domestic market.

Lyons was very thorough and extremely focused. He had witnessed the damage that could be wrought through the kind of scatter-gun approach that had almost brought Ocelot to its knees and he was not about to repeat it. He narrowed his field down to Gabon and Tanzania and did a development deal with some current onshore oil production in Gabon and a similar offshore gas deal in Tanzania. Neither was expensive. It was this point that a brief report on the company crossed Geoffrey Scott's desk.

Geoffrey quickly established that Pan Ocean's cash position equated almost exactly to its share price and that it had no debt. He immediately called Peter but, if he had been expecting an immediate buy order, he was disappointed. It was at just that moment that Cable & Wireless was beginning to unravel and Peter was consequently very wary of cash pools in the hands of management groups about which he knew little, in industries with a capacity to devour cash – in his book oil exploration and development was just such a one. However, he felt obligated to pursue the investigation and he wasted very little time in doing so. He met with David Lyons in Vancouver within weeks and was immediately impressed. This was a cautious and disciplined entrepreneur, who was dealing with a pool of cash that in large measure was his own. In Peter's opinion, he would husband it with great care so that the chances of his blowing it on reckless adventure seemed remote.

But he was not yet convinced that Lyon's international strategy, with its focus on Gabon and Tanzania, was likely to create significant additional shareholder value. Peter was not reticent about expressing his doubts. Lyon's response was to say that there was only one way to arrive at a fair assessment – Peter should visit the Gabon project to see for himself – and he offered to sponsor him.

It was a shrewd call on Lyon's part. He was speaking to an inveterate globe trotter with boundless curiosity and a taste for adventure. By the beginning of July Peter was on his way in the company of Brittany Lyons, David's daughter, and David Roberts, Pan Ocean's head of operations in Gabon:

> David Roberts is a thirty-four-year-old graduate of the Colorado School of Mines and, young though he is, the veteran of many overseas assignments. He is a man of charm and humour, but beware if your on-site housekeeping is not up to scratch. His French is terrific. He was sent to the interior of Gabon to oversee a crew without a word. Six months later he was fluent.

They flew to Libreville and then on down to Port Gentil, where Albert Schweitzer built his hospital in 1926. Peter did his usual run around the city getting a sense of neatness, relative prosperity, and an air of contentment among the townsfolk. The following morning:

We donned orange overalls and work boots. After a bit of a false start we climbed aboard a helicopter to make the forty minute trip to the Orangue onshore field. David Roberts was livid about the quality of the housekeeping. Heads rolled. To my untutored eye, it was a lot neater than the rigs in Western Siberia. We toured the area on the logging roads, stopping at a local village on the river. It was not an advert for *Town and Country* but for West Africa....!

Next morning we helicoptered to the offshore Etame site, dropping off a guy from Marathon Oil on their jack-up rig on the way. Etame is serviced by a tanker converted in Singapore for the purpose. Production is gathered from the wells and connected to the FPSO (floating production storage off-take), which can hold over a million barrels. Tankers offload the oil from the stationary holding vessel. It is a big mother. The captain is Polish, the chief engineer Indian, and most of the thirty-strong crew Philippino. We had a fine tour and lunch. We were in cloudbanks coming out, so we hugged the coastline on the way home to Libreville looking for elephants.

In the morning Peter took a tour of the capital guided by a young Gabonese employee of Pan Ocean; a well-informed, articulate law graduate:

Saw President Bongo's palace, a busy but orderly marketplace, the industrial zone and the railway station which brings in magnesium from the eastern part of Gabon. The headquarters of the West African Central Bank is here. I conclude that Gabon is rich, although it is also in default on a slice of publicly traded debt. Bongo ran a one party state until 1990, then there were riots and now the opposition is recognized – a form of democracy exists. Bongo is obviously not a vicious dictator, rather something of a pragmatist – he converted to Islam [from Christianity] and promptly married five wives. He has a comfortable lifestyle, but enough of the largesse filters down.

This is a stable place, the cars are modern, and the drivers are disciplined. I never felt threatened or uncomfortable. There are mercenaries and the French Foreign Legion to keep the peace. Except for President Bongo, most of the population is Christian and there is one major tribe and a dialect.

Notwithstanding his favourable impression, Peter watched the shares of Pan Ocean ticking upwards little by little for another five months before he actually bought any. In the fall of the following year David Lyons persuaded Peter that he ought to check out Tanzania as well, rounding out the African experience with a few days in the Okavango Valley at the end.

We flew to Dar es Salaam, a city with a population of over a million out of a total population of 37 million. The city centre is ordered, with a good bit of construction in progress, but the country is poor. Per capita GNP is just over $600.

We flew on down to Songo Songo where the gas was discovered and developed. The project of moving gas to the Ubungo power plant in Dar has been on the drawing board since '76. To date the power plants have been mostly hydro. Recently there have been serious droughts and the reservoirs are now dangerously low. The gas solution has now become urgent, hence the completion of the $250 million project. We were invited to the opening reception hosted by the president. Ministers and senior civil servants seemed energetic and able. The country is stable and has turned away from its extreme socialist past.

The Tanzanian stock market is nascent – just seven companies, five of which have 9% dividend yields, P/E's under 10, and, better still, trade well below book. Unfortunately there's a foreign ownership cap, which rules us out for the moment. Tanzania Breweries is impressive and uses Songa gas.

Peter spent four days hopping around the Okavango in a light aircraft. A place called Gudigwa, home to the Bukakwe San bushmen, was the highlight.

When we had our bushman dinner, the witch doctor danced. As long as he stayed doing the shimmy I had no difficulty keeping up. Then he started to hop on one foot and I followed – not so wise. The music and the chanting were completely captivating.

I shall never forget the African sunsets, particularly at altitude. The sun moves on a downward path rather briskly, emitting strong primary colours. We would stop the Land Rover for a "sundowner" and watch the powerful pull of the struggle between the day and the night. It is a brief moment, but compelling, and it sums up my view of Africa.

Peter ended up owning about 6% of Pan Ocean. He made six times his money in two and a half years, finally selling out on a bid from the Chinese.

18

The Russian Bear

PETER MADE HIS FIRST VISIT to Russia in 1993, early in Boris Yeltsin's reign as the first president of the Russian Federation and before the formation of the Moscow stock exchange. He had concluded then that there was nothing he could do until a more reliable commercial and legal framework emerged, with at least some semblance of Western accounting. He visited again in 1997 and summarized his impressions of the changes he saw:

> This is still a society in transition and confusion buttressed by some substantial economic progress. The most compelling change is that now about 65% of the work-force is in the private sector – up from 3% in '91. There have been three waves of capitalists so far. The first were the "King Rats," fast-moving entrepreneurs who took what they could grab and ran to more hospitable climes. The second were the thugs who filled the vacuum left by the breakdown of control from legitimate government. We saw the third wave of earnest, young males, well-educated types. They are learning the language of corporate governance and process. This will take time to mature. There is still a numbing, arbitrary, and inefficient bureaucracy.

> A Western investor is at substantial risk that the rules of the game will simply be changed at the stroke of a pen, sometimes retroactively. The level of theoretical taxation is so high that if you were to play it straight you would go broke personally and corporately. Cheating is a fact of survival.
>
> As we all know, the Russian share market has been on a roll. Valuations are still modest. The entire market trades at around book value, four times cash flow and nine times earnings. The dividend yield is negligible. Debt is not high and if one assumes growth, one could invest. But, and here's the rub, on balance, there seems to be a Russian crisis every eighteen months. The next one will be the state of the central government's finances and it cannot be far off.
>
> I shall continue to explore possible investment in Russia, but I am in no hurry. The margin of safety is not in place.

Peter was spot on. The Russian debt crisis occurred less than a year later. It sent shock waves around the world and caused the collapse of a large and well known hedge fund, Long Term Capital Management. It had an impact on all financial markets, not just Russia.

However, crisis always signalled opportunity in Peter's shorthand. Prior to the debt default he had noticed that a Russian oil company, Sibir Energy, had the distinction of being, by some margin, the largest company listed on the London Stock Exchange's Alternative Investment Market (AIM). Sibir's capitalization was then significantly bigger than many companies with a full London listing. In the wake of the crisis Sibir's share price had plummeted, along with every other Russian stock, and Peter was curious to discover whether this was attributable to the overall panic or whether Sibir was confronting some fundamental corporate difficulties and he asked James Morton to have a look at it.

What James's research revealed was more than a little interesting. Sibir had been founded in 1996 and obtained an AIM listing on the London Stock Exchange the following year. It owned a UK operation that was cash flow positive and worth approximately half the company's market capitalization. It had a rag bag of assets in Italy, whose value probably represented another quarter, which left a collection of assets in Russia, including one mature oilfield that was also cash flow positive and worth between 25% and 50% of the market cap.

The rest of the assets were thrown in for free. But the most important elements of the package were a 50% interest in two oilfields, both in Siberia, one in partnership with Sibneft, controlled by Roman Abramovich, and the other a rather loosely constructed joint venture with Shell.

At this period it was fashionable to denigrate all seismic work on Russia's hydrocarbon deposits conducted prior to the establishment of the Federation. However, James took the trouble to get hold of the old Soviet data on the two fields. Although not considered admissible by AIM market standards, or indeed GAAP (generally accepted accounting principles)-friendly, James felt that the data was sufficiently professional to enable him to make a very fair estimate of Sibir's share in the recoverable reserves. It added up to about 1 billion barrels, a significant portion of which could be developed for production quite quickly.

Looking at the sum of the parts from that standpoint James calculated that you were paying a mere 10 cents per barrel in the ground for the Russian reserves, well below the value of any other listed Russian oil company. Quite obviously this represented a considerable margin of safety. Peter, however, remained to be convinced as he believed that nothing in Russia was ever straightforward; this certainly proved to be the case with Sibir.

Nevertheless, he made another trip to Russia in the spring of 1999 at the invitation of Brunswick Capital Management and used the opportunity to visit Khanty-Mansiysk in Siberia – the oil capital of Russia:

> K-M is located some 2,000 km north-east of Moscow. It was settled by political prisoners in the '30s and now boasts a population of some 45,000. Oil was discovered in the '60s and developed until the early '90s with production reaching 15 million barrels a day – now down to 6 million due to underinvestment and antiquated technology. We visited KMOC, which has roughly a billion barrels of proven and probable reserves. Drilling is developmental, not exploratory. Relative to its price a billion barrels is interesting, but not compelling. There are others, including Sibir, that have similar interests close by and are cheaper.
>
> We visited a rig by helicopter. I was none the wiser but I was impressed in other ways. The local hotel was spartan but clean. The food was simple and hearty. The people were well dressed. I saw one woman in a fur coat that was well cut and had real style. Modern flats are going up, replacing the old wooden huts. Taxes are being paid here: the region is wealthy. A regional investment fund has been created, similar to Alberta. There is an art collection bought at Sotheby's. A biathlon range for the 2003 world championships is being built. But where is the opera house!?

On his return Peter told James that he thought Sibir might be worth a "punt" in the Mackenzie Cundill Recovery Fund. James set to work immediately with Cannacord, the brokers who had sponsored Sibir's

AIM listing. Sibir was hungry for investment capital and seemed disposed to accept it on very favourable terms for the investor. What they negotiated was a small private placement in the form of a convertible debenture at a small premium to the market – a negligible price to pay, the shares having fallen from 47p the previous June, prior to the Russian crisis, to 10p. In addition to giving them a preferential position over the common equity there was a 12% coupon. It was a small issue in which, with $5 million, they were the largest player, but it gave them an initial stake for the Recovery Fund at an advantageous price with a built-in margin of safety.

It was, nevertheless, to be a bumpy ride. Everything that could go wrong did. Shell tried to squeeze Sibir out of the Salyn oil field by accelerating the cash requirements to bring it on stream to a level it believed Sibir would be unable to support. Sibir's largest shareholder, Chalva Tchigirinski, who was in a successful real estate partnership with, among others, the mayor of Moscow's wife, loaned Sibir enough to plug the gap and Shell was eventually obliged to drop its hard-ball tactics. Sibir still had to sell off its UK and Italian assets to fund its Russian developments.

Next Sibir succeeded in vastly increasing its risk by getting involved in a struggle with the "big boys." By this time Sibir had acquired an interest in a small chain of petrol stations in Moscow in a joint venture with BP and it had a claim to a controlling interest in the Moscow Oil and Gas Refinery, the strategic refiner for the Moscow region with no other competition within a 150 mile radius of the city. The strength of the legal title to this refinery appeared to rest on a personal relationship between Tchigirinski and the mayor of Moscow, or, perhaps more pertinently, the mayor's wife. Its adversaries were LukOil and Sibneft, then owned by Roman Abramovich, whose angelic face belies a steely determination to achieve his ends, as well as a robustly

Russian approach to doing so. In alliance with Tchigirinski and the mayor, Sibir fought the battle in and out of court and emerged successful. It was an important strategic victory because control of the refinery enabled Sibir to sell its production domestically at a significant premium. At the time pipeline capacity for the export of Russian oil was considerably less than the ability of the fields to pump the barrels and the domestic market was not sufficiently developed to be able to absorb the balance except at very low prices. The Urals discount on the world price was at times as high as 50%. The realized net price for the refined product from oil sold to the Moscow refinery was much closer to the international price, so that the value of the quota for processing oil through the refinery was much greater than Sibir's asset value. But in achieving this control Sibir had put some powerful noses out of joint and the retaliation was swift and ruthless.

Through the mechanism of a series of very extraordinary Extraordinary General Meetings of the partnership group, about which they had not been informed, Sibir's management woke up one day to discover that their 50% interest in the Siberian joint venture with Sibneft had been unaccountably diluted down to 1%. At the same time certain elements within ministries in Moscow began a series of attempts to confiscate the Salyn oil licence on a variety of spurious grounds, although it ultimately failed. Possibly suspecting that Sibir was an unhelpful associate for a company wishing to do business with the Russian state, BP tried to back out of its retail deal.

All of this turmoil created huge volatility in the Sibir share price, which James Morton exploited to advantage, running and rerunning the "sum of the parts" calculations to reassure himself and Peter that the margin of safety was still intact. It always was. In fact even at the peaks Sibir's shares never traded at above 40% of the "sum of the parts." By 2006 the capital gain was five times the investment and in addition James had traded it extremely deftly, enhancing the return to 40% per annum from 30%. Once it became clear that Sibir was not going to be forced into bankruptcy Shell turned into an exemplary partner in the Salyn field, which began to provide substantial cash flow, enabling Sibir to accumulate a considerable cash pile.

But the drama still had one more act. By 2008 Tchigirinski's real estate operations in Moscow were in serious trouble and he was running out of cash. He invited Henry Cameron, Sibir's well-respected CEO, to a meeting at his villa in the South of France. It must be supposed that Tchigirinski intimated to Cameron that it was now pay-back time. This time it was he who required a lifeline. No doubt he represented it as being a very short-term emergency and he may have believed that was the case. Cameron was no fool and must have weighed up the situation as a pragmatist with a Russian hat on. The upshot was that the better part of $500 million left Sibir's bank accounts for Tchigirinski's, ostensibly as consideration for his Moscow real estate assets. This would have transformed Sibir from an oil and gas production company into a quasi property company. When the news of the proposed transaction was eventually broken to the rest of Sibir's board, they refused to authorize it. Unfortunately the cash never reappeared and, when this became known, Sibir was suspended from the AIM market and Cameron was summarily fired. Tchigirinski simply disappeared, but bailiffs seized his villa in the South of France, impounded his boats and aircraft, and his Eaton Square home in London was sold for £33 million.

The value of Sibir was impaired but far from destroyed. A case could still be made for a break-up value well in excess of £10 per share and oil prices were reaching ever dizzier heights. It was, nevertheless, Sibir's weakest moment. Its jugular was exposed and the wolf pack was circling. Renaissance, the Russian investment bank, moved very swiftly, no doubt anticipating that Sibir's shareholders would be running scared and hoping to secure a kill before anyone else could react.

They launched a tender offer at a derisory £2.00 per share and might have succeeded but for Richard Fennels, a lawyer by training, and ex-chief executive of Ansbacher, a City of London merchant bank, now with his own corporate finance boutique and a string of excellent Russian connections. He went straight to the top people at Gazprom Neft, the fifth largest oil producing and refining company in Russia, whom he knew well, and with great skill persuaded them that a knock-out offer to pre-empt anyone else was required. To the immense surprise of many of Sibir's shareholders, and the relief of nearly all of them, what followed was a clincher bid at £5.00 per share.

Neither Peter nor James was inclined to wait around to pick up the 20p premium available to the "risk arbitrageurs" and the entire position was sold into the "grey market" at £4.80. The Sibir investment had finally turned into a "ten bagger." If ever there was an illustration of the efficacy of a solid margin of safety, it had to be this. But the rising oil price had done no harm either. The whole saga had been an enormously valuable learning curve whose worth probably far outweighed the, albeit handsome, investment return. It had prepared the ground for a number of other successful investments, particularly by the Recovery Fund, in the more outlandish extremities of the old republics of the Soviet Union. It had given them real insights into how it was possible to generate very substantial profits in post-Soviet transitional economies without being exposed to unacceptable levels of risk. What was required was an asset-based margin of safety significantly greater than would be considered adequate in the more developed markets. It was also fairly obvious that in these less developed markets tangible fixed assets were superior to cash, which had a nasty habit of evaporating.

19

The Canadian Buffett

PETER FIRST MET PREM WATSA back in the 1980s when Prem was an executive at the Confederation Life Insurance Company in Toronto. As they got to know each other they discovered that they had a great deal in common. Like Peter, Prem is a convinced and practising disciple of Benjamin Graham, an admirer of Warren Buffett, and counted Sir John Templeton as a friend, counsellor on many levels, and business mentor. Also in common with Peter, Prem regularly visited Sir John in Nassau and enjoyed his confidence. Sir John was a shareholder of Fairfax Financial, Prem's company, as well as a unit holder of the Cundill Value Fund.

Peter had been a firm admirer of Prem's for many years and the respect was mutual. However, on strict value principles he had never found it possible to buy shares in Fairfax since it had never sold below book value; that is, not until 2000. By 1995, after ten years in business under Prem's stewardship, Fairfax consisted of six insurance companies, an investment management firm, a claims adjusting company, and a Bermuda-based reinsurer. The holding company was extremely profitable and Prem had acquired a reputation for buying up good companies with short term problems that he knew he could fix – and paying a low price to book value. The Fairfax share price had risen over the period from $3.75 to $80.

Between 1995 and 1998 Fairfax went on the acquisition trail as never before, adding Swedish-owned Skandia American Insurance, which doubled its assets. This was followed by Compagnie Transcontinentale de Réassurance, financed by a private placement at a premium to the Fairfax share price. In 1998 there were two more purchases, this time financed with debt to the tune of three times Fairfax's shareholders' equity: Crum and Forster Holdings, a Xerox subsidiary that had been on the block for some time so it came at a good price, although with the usual set of problems, and TIG Holdings, both of them serving the US commercial market with TIG specialized in New York.

Investors were enthused about this series of acquisitions and the integration appeared to be proceeding well and according to plan. However 1999 ushered in a season of abnormally severe storms in Europe, resulting in very high catastrophe losses at the same time that investment returns started to falter in the wake of the Russian debt crisis and the failure of the hedge fund Long-Term Capital Management. Underwriting performance was severely hurt and Fairfax's return on equity fell below 20% for the second year running. The share price suffered, falling from $228 to $164, below book value for the first time in the company's history and into Peter's sights. In the spring of 2000 Peter bought $122 million of Fairfax at an average price of $171. It was the biggest single position that any Mackenzie equity fund had ever had.

In the soul-searching that had followed the Cable & Wireless loss, Peter had suggested that with respect to any investment where the CIR group were unanimously favourable, there was a strong case for appointing a devil's advocate to argue a contrary view. In the Fairfax case that would have been quite unnecessary: CIR had recently acquired a bright new analyst who was anxious to make his mark. He was given the responsibility of following the Fairfax investment on a day to day basis and he set about doing so with a vengeance, concluding that there was a very high probability Fairfax could run into difficulty. Neither Peter, nor Tim McElvaine, who ran the Mackenzie Cundill Canadian Security Fund, nor Wade Burton, who oversaw the Canadian investments of the main Value Fund, was greatly bothered. They were convinced that there was a very adequate margin of safety within the assemblage of Fairfax's assets, without which it would not have been bought. However, the young man was both persistent and voluble on the subject and so, when the stock spiked up again nine months later, Peter cut the position in half at an average of $217.

It was a fortuitous decision, although not for the reasons advanced by his young colleague. 9/11 intervened, hitting TIG, with its New York bias, especially hard and tipping Fairfax into loss for the first time ever. Despite Fairfax being more than adequately capitalized, particularly as a result of the IPO of Odyssey RE, its main reinsurance vehicle, which had netted the parent company over $400 million, the share price plummeted. Peter stayed with the position, relying on his estimate of Prem's ability to steer Fairfax out of troubled waters and on the detailed asset analysis put together and continuously updated by Wade Burton.

Peter's confidence was fully justified as Prem did an about-face on Fairfax's strategy of growth through acquisition to focus on internal growth and a drive for new business to pull in the premiums. The change of tack was very quickly rewarded. Not only did Fairfax return to profitability in 2002, it made the largest profit in its history – $415 million, attributed by Prem to a combination of positive response to the sales push in the form of an influx of premiums as well as above average investment returns. Initially the shares bounced back sharply to over $200.

However, as with all myths of invincibility, it takes just a single reverse to shatter the illusion. Investors had not really regained their confidence and negative rumours about Fairfax abounded, most of them with scant foundation or riddled with inaccuracies. The problem, however, was that at this juncture investors were prepared to listen and the bears were out in force. The stock price began to drift downward again.

Fairfax pipped up to another peak in earnings in 2003 but this was followed by two years of losses. These were industry-wide, as a result of the worst hurricane seasons in US history, but for Fairfax no excuses were acceptable. Ordinary bears had metamorphosed into a pack of aggressive short sellers intent on destroying the company if they could. Within CIR Wade Burton remained Fairfax's staunchest ally, supported by Peter, whose confidence in Prem was still amply reinforced by his conviction that the sum of the parts calculation provided a more than adequate margin of safety. When he was approached to lend out his stock in Fairfax, clearly in order to facilitate the short sellers, he refused emphatically and, as the shares fell back from $200 to just above $100 in 2005 and 2006, the investment was more than doubled. It was added to again in early 2007.

By this time there was an additional reason for the holding. In his letter to shareholders accompanying the Fairfax annual report in 2004 Prem had enunciated his doubts about securitized products.

> We have been concerned for some time about the risks in asset backed bonds, particularly those backed by home equity loans (we own no asset backed bonds). It seems to us that the creation of these asset backed bonds eliminates the incentive for the originator of the loan to be credit sensitive ... With securitization, the dealer [almost] does not care as these loans can be

> laid off through securitization. Thus, the loss experienced on these loans after securitization will no longer be comparable to that experienced prior to securitization. This is not a small problem. There is $1 trillion in asset backed bonds outstanding. Who is buying these bonds? Insurance companies, money managers, and banks – in the main – all reaching for the yield given the excellent ratings for these bonds. What happens if we hit an air pocket?

At that time the reassurance that Fairfax was clean of such instruments gave Peter additional comfort with respect to the solidity of his margin of safety in the company. However by 2006, as the banks' leverage ratcheted up from 10:1 to 50:1, Peter was as deeply concerned about the time bomb in the financial system as Prem.

During the early 1990s a new instrument had emerged, known as a Credit Default Swap: in effect an instrument that allowed the purchaser to protect himself against the default of any traded instrument in exchange for the payment of a fairly small "premium," or spread, over the relevant Treasury Bill rate. By purchasing "naked" CDS's, that is without actually owning the instrument against whose default one was purchasing protection, one could speculate against any credit. Prem was by then supremely pessimistic about the likelihood of a major financial catastrophe caused by a collapse in the securitized bond market and had begun to buy "naked" CDS's on this class of paper very aggressively. Although equally pessimistic, Peter was not permitted to do this in a mutual fund, so that the most effective way in which he could back his judgement was to participate by proxy through owning shares in Fairfax.

By the end of September 2007 Fairfax and its subsidiaries owned a credit default swap book with an $18.5 billion dollar nominal amount on about thirty companies, most of which were bond insurers and mortgage lenders. The book had a cost of $344 million. As the events of 2008 unfolded, these CDS positions matured into one of the great investment calls of all time. From June 2006 to date the Fairfax share price has risen from just over $100 to over $400. As at 30 September 2010 the share price was $417 and the Mackenzie Cundill Value Fund still held 537,106 shares.

20

Fragile X

AS EARLY AS 1998 PETER had begun to notice that he was developing a slight tremor, particularly affecting his right arm. Initially he thought little of it, but by the early 2000s it had started to become more troublesome and had spread to his left arm as well. The initial diagnosis was confused, suggesting either that Peter was exhibiting the early symptoms of Parkinson's disease or that he had developed a vague condition referred to as "benign tremor." He was treated with Parkinson's medication, to which he did not respond at all. His shaking became much more severe and he began to have problems with his balance. Despite this he was, as always, leading a full and exceptionally active business and social life, with an exercise regime of which a man in his thirties might have been proud.

However, by the end of 2005, while it was perfectly clear that Peter's investment acumen was as sharp as ever and his presentational skills unimpaired, Charles Sims (Charlie), Mackenzie's new CEO as successor to Jim Hunter, was becoming concerned that, if the deterioration in Peter's condition were to continue at this rate, it might quite soon become impossible for Peter to carry on the management of the large and important Mackenzie Cundill group of funds.

Peter had, of course, already given thought to the question of a successor and had built up the team within Cundill Investment Research with the idea that it would be the cradle from which the right individual would emerge, fully equipped and moulded into the Graham and Dodd value framework as he had developed it. That said, Peter had never envisaged retiring at the conventional age of sixty-five. His old friend Irving Kahn was still working at over a hundred and Al Gordon, of Kidder fame, had carried on well into his eighties. Peter's father had lived till he was eighty-six and his mother to ninety-three. Both of them had remained fully alert and active into their mid eighties. On the face of it there was good reason to think that he might continue his working life for many years to come, especially as he was so extraordinarily fit. Investment is Peter's primary passion and he had already written rather starkly in his journal, "retirement is a death warrant."

But the outlook for Peter changed drastically as his physical condition began to visibly deteriorate at the end of 2004. It had to be recognized that the time-line for Peter's fully active working life had shortened substantially. Charlie Sims came to the conclusion that the best way to secure the future of the Mackenzie Cundill funds – safeguarding the interests of both the unit-holders and Mackenzie – would be to bring the whole Cundill operation fully under Mackenzie's control and integrate it within the group. This would ensure, when the time came that Peter was no longer able to carry on, that there was no hiatus but a seamless transfer of responsibility to the portfolio manager designated as his successor and that Mackenzie would be in a position to participate directly in that selection process.

Talks began immediately between Peter and Charlie. The terms were quickly agreed and on 8 August 2006 Mackenzie announced that it would be acquiring Cundill Investment Research and all its related businesses. Peter and his team would, henceforward, become employees of Mackenzie. It was understood between Peter and Charlie that Peter would continue to oversee the management of all the funds and the institutional portfolios, with Mackenzie's full support, for as long as he felt able to do so. At the same time Mackenzie would begin a focused initiative that would eventually lead to the nomination or recruitment of Peter's successor.

Ironically, just as Peter's health began to decline an increasing number of industry awards for his achievements started to come his way. In 2001 he collected the "Fund Manager of the Year" award from *Investment Executive*, Canada's newspaper for financial advisors. In December of the same year he was honoured at the Canadian Mutual Fund Awards Gala dinner attended by six hundred investment professionals. Billed as the highlight of the night and described as the "Indiana Jones of Fund Managers," he received the Analyst's Choice award as "The Greatest Mutual Fund Manager of All Time." He rounded off his conventional acceptance speech unexpectedly with a poem composed for the occasion:

> But Hark,
> Listen to the clarion call,
> Duty and trust,
> Excitement and risk,
> Comradeship and challenge,
> We all of us have moments in the sun
> And moments in the shade,
> No fortunes are made in prosperity,
> Ours is a marathon without end:
> Enjoy the passing moments.

Again in 2003 he received the Fund Manager of the Year Award at the Canadian Investment Awards. In 2004 he was elected a Fellow Chartered Accountant. At the presentation ceremony it was stated the he had "excelled in a way few of us can ever imagine and, in the process, has influenced a generation of investment managers while at the same time creating wealth for his investors."

At the end of 2006 Canadian industry analysts chose the Mackenzie Cundill Value Fund as the winner of the award for the best global equity fund. The award coincided with a final correct diagnosis of Peter's condition as Fragile X-associated tremor/ataxia syndrome (FXTAS), a degenerative neurological disorder for which there is as yet no effective treatment.

The issue of succession was not entirely straightforward. Peter's were big boots to fill and the requirements were complex. The job demanded a complete understanding of deep value investment combined with long term experience in its practice. Leadership skills needed to be considered because, while Cundill Investment Research was a team effort, Peter had always led from the front, giving direction on every aspect of managing the portfolios and remaining central to the formulation of strategy and intimately involved in every investment decision. The net-net worksheets that he had devised in the seventies formed the backbone of the analytical process, as they still do today. The international aspect was important too because most of the Mackenzie Cundill funds are in global equities.

But, more than just a familiarity with global investing, it would require a well conceived effort to maintain and to continue to build upon the world-wide network of contacts and associations that Peter had established over thirty years. Although Vancouver had remained CIR's headquarters, Peter was rarely there. He ran the team by keeping in daily contact from wherever he might be and it would have been naive to suppose that a similar arrangement would work for anyone else.

The group of eight portfolio managers in 2006 was hugely talented but there was no single individual who combined all the desirable attributes and Peter recognized this. He had always been a generous and effective mentor who found it a pleasure to nurture talent; now he made it his business to foster a culture of far greater independence, encouraging his team to regard him as a counsellor or chairman rather than a chief executive. The result was that by 2009, when Peter felt that it was no longer feasible for him to continue, the CIR team had grown in stature so that it was more than sufficiently ready to be able to take over seamlessly.

As might have been expected, the two people who emerged in leading roles had both been with Peter for many years: Andy Massie, who had joined in 1984 and had had primary portfolio responsibility for the Value Fund since 2004, and Lawrence Chin, who had joined in 1999 and was responsible for the Canadian funds. At the end of April 2009 Peter stepped down, relinquishing all day-to-day responsibility and assuming the honorific title of Chairman Emeritus Mackenzie Cundill Investment Management Ltd.

Although Peter no longer has any formal role, it is interesting to note that even now, eighteen months later, Andy Massie calls Peter weekly to discuss what they are doing and canvass his views. James Morton visits him at home every three or four weeks for the same purpose. Peter remains a voracious reader. His unfailing daily diet consists of the *Wall Street Journal*, the *Financial Times*, the *Times* and the *International Herald Tribune*. He also reads *Barron's*, the *Economist*, the *Spectator*, the *Week*, the *New Yorker*, and the *Financial Post* and the *Globe and Mail* on Saturdays.

21

What Makes a Great Investor?

FROM THE HUGE "CORPUS" of Peter's writing – the journals, the investment notebooks, the thousands of memos and research notes as well as transcripts of speeches – it seemed that it would be a worthwhile exercise to try to distil what, in the final analysis, Peter himself believes constitute the characteristics that are common to most great investors. They are given in no particular order and it does not seem that Peter has ever sought to prioritize them either. Nevertheless, there are two characteristics that appear in his writings and speeches with greater frequency than all the rest.

INSATIABLE CURIOSITY

"Curiosity is the engine of civilization. If I were to elaborate it would be to say read, read, read, and don't forget to talk to people, really talk, listening with attention and having conversations, on whatever topic, that are an exchange of thoughts. Keep the reading broad, beyond just the professional. This helps to develop one's sense of perspective in all matters."

PATIENCE

"Patience, patience, and more patience. Ben Graham said it,

but it is true of all investment disciplines, not only value investing, although it is indispensable to that."

CONCENTRATION

"You must have the ability to focus and to block out distractions. I am talking about not getting carried away by events or outside influences – you can take them into account, but you must stick to your framework."

ATTENTION TO DETAIL

"Never make the mistake of not reading the small print, no matter how rushed you are. Always read the notes to a set of accounts very carefully – they are your barometer. You need sound simple arithmetic skills, not differential calculus. They will give you the ability to spot patterns without a calculator or a spread sheet. Seeing the patterns will develop your investment insights, your instincts – your sense of smell. Eventually it will give you the agility to stay ahead of the game, making quick, reasoned decisions, especially in a crisis.

CALCULATED RISK

"Be prepared to take risks but never gambles. Value investors are often perceived as taking the safe investment route and that is true. But the time scales required for a value investor can be contradictory. Holding on to heavily discounted stock that the market dislikes for a period of five or ten years is not risk free. As each year passes the required end reward to justify the investment becomes higher, irrespective of the original margin of safety. Equally for the growth specialist, speculating that a company in a favoured market, with negligible current earnings, will in due course enjoy exponential growth is not risk free. On top of which there is no margin of safety. Either could be regarded as gambling, or calculated risk. Which side of that scale they fall on is a function of whether the homework has been good enough and has not neglected the fieldwork."

INDEPENDENCE OF MIND

"I think it is very useful to develop a contrarian cast of mind combined with a keen sense of what I would call "the natural order of things." If you can cultivate these two attributes you are unlikely to become infected by dogma and you will begin to have a predisposition towards lateral thinking – making important connections intuitively."

HUMILITY

"I have no doubt that a strong sense of self belief is important – even a sense of mission – and this is fine as long as it is tempered by a sense of humour, especially an ability to laugh at oneself. One of the greatest dangers that confront those who have been through a period of successful investment is hubris – the conviction that one can never be wrong again. An ability to see the funny side of oneself as it is seen by others is a strong antidote to hubris."

ROUTINES

"Routines and discipline go hand in hand. They are the roadmap that guides the pursuit of excellence for its own sake. They support proper professional ambition and the commercial integrity that goes with it."

MENS SANA IN CORPORE SANO

"I know that there are successful investors who are supremely unfit and don't give a fig. For myself I have found that my exercise routines have contributed immensely towards giving me the mental resilience to get through the tough times – and there always are tough times. I also believe that engaging in competitive sport has taught me to temper my competitive instincts with common sense and only to attempt what I sincerely think is possible – that works professionally too. About fifty percent of my time is spent reading and running is useful for digesting it all. I run almost every day, but I hope not to the point of obsession. I have been known to have the odd dry martini now and then! But I am convinced that there is a strong link in temperament between elite athletes and elite investors. Watching the best sportsmen in action prompts the question as to why the best are so much better than everyone else. Perhaps it is because they practise "adaptive perfectionism." This is something that is readily applicable to investment and I have tried to follow it by remaining faithful to the Ben Graham principles that I believe are the soundest route to investment success, while retaining an eye for adapting them and moving them forward to fit today's investment world more perfectly."

SCEPTICISM

"Scepticism is good, but be a sceptic, not an iconoclast. Have rigour and flexibility, which might be considered an oxymoron but is exactly what I meant when I quoted Peter Robertson's dictum 'always change a winning game.' An investment framework ought to include a liberal dose of scepticism both in terms of markets and of company accounts. Taking this a step further, a lot of MBA programs, particularly these days, teach you about market efficiency and accounting rules, but this is not a perfect world and there will always be anomalies and there is always "wriggle room" within company accounts so you have to stick to your guns and forget the hype."

PERSONAL RESPONSIBILITY

"The ability to shoulder personal responsibility for one's investment results is pretty fundamental. This means that if you lose money it isn't the market's fault, it isn't some broker's fault, and it isn't the fault of your research department or anyone else. It is in fact the direct result of your own decisions. Coming to terms with this reality sets you free to learn from your mistakes."

READING AGAIN

"There are a few books – really not that many – which I believe are indispensable reading for every serious investor in whatever facet of investment practice they may favour:

- *Extraordinary Popular Delusions and the Madness of Crowds* by Charles Mackay (only the first two chapters – the title is worth the price of admission!)
- *The Crowd: A Study of the Popular Mind* by Gustave Le Bon
- *Buffett: The Making of an American Capitalist* by Roger Lowenstein
- *The Money Masters* by John Train
- *The Intelligent Investor: A Book of Practical Counsel* by Benjamin Graham
- *The Templeton Touch* by William Proctor
- *The Alchemy of Finance* by George Soros

22

A Kind of Retirement

IF PETER HAD EVER IMAGINED that retirement would constitute a hiatus in activity, he was mistaken. He had not given up travelling and wherever he happened to be he continued to receive a constant stream of visitors, business and social, on top of which there was the Cundill History Prize. Peter had founded this in 2007 through McGill University, his alma mater. It is the largest history prize in the world and as well as being international – of the first two winners one, Stuart Schwartz, is American and the second, Lisa Jardine, is British – is devoted to academic works that are both accessible to a general readership and in some way break new ground.

Although not a member of the jury, nor desirous of exerting any influence on its deliberations, Peter receives all the short-listed books – usually between ten and twelve a year out of the hundreds entered – looks at all of them, and reads those that particularly take his fancy as well as the winning work. He also likes to communicate with the authors and his comments are stimulating and trenchant. Nor has he in any way relinquished his passionate interest in investment.

He has put in place a family office to manage his own affairs that is a model of efficiency, located in Bermuda. In terms of the investment of his personal fortune, he decided at the end of last year to give a mandate to his old friend and business associate Richard Oldfield of Oldfield Partners.

Richard, nevertheless, knows Peter too well to assume that this affords him a free hand. For the moment, it is more of a consultative role in which Richard does the legwork that Peter is no longer able to undertake and makes cautious and well-presented suggestions that he then discusses with Peter in detail. It is a process in the development of a new relationship and of a fuller understanding of Peter's long-term objectives for what will be a very important charitable foundation. The character of the investment portfolio has unquestionably been totally determined by Peter. It will come as no surprise that the equity portion of it is entirely composed of funds invested on value principles, run by managers whom Peter has known and admired for many years and funds run by those who have worked for him or whom he has in some way mentored. The two largest positions on the equity side remain the Mackenzie Cundill Value Fund run by Andy Massie and the Cundill International Company Ltd run by James Morton under Mackenzie Cundill Investment Mgmt (Bermuda) Ltd. (There is a complete list of the funds represented in the portfolios that form the body of the Cundill private investments in Appendix 2.)

On the fixed interest side there is only one significant manager, Mark Coombs's Ashmore Group. Peter has a very substantial amount invested in the Ashmore Emerging Markets Corporate High Yield Fund. Peter has a relationship with Mark Coombs that goes back many years to the period when Mark was running the emerging market debt division at ANZ Bank, before he bought out that division and formed Ashmore.

In the aftermath of the stock market crash of 2008, the Peter Cundill Trust was sitting on a very considerable amount of cash that was attracting derisory interest. By early 2009 Peter was convinced that the worst of the economic and financial crisis was over and that disaster had been averted, although only just. At his suggestion the Trust had already increased its position in equity funds – notably with a large additional purchase in Cundill International Company Ltd – and he felt that this was now sufficient equity exposure.

At the same time Peter's restlessly contrarian brain had not been idle and his thinking had crystallized. In his view short term interest rates were likely to remain close to zero for some time to come; certainly until the economic recovery had shown itself to be thoroughly robust over a fairly extended period. The longer maturities of the sovereign debt of countries with good credit ratings was of scarcely greater attraction than the short end and the interest-spread differential between the debt of triple A rated countries and countries carrying a relatively high risk of default was totally inadequate to justify their additional risk.

What did seem clear to Peter was that, on the assumption that the economic recovery, albeit somewhat anaemic, was for real, the corporate debt of companies that had been having a difficult trading time but whose balance sheets were relatively unimpaired might offer the chance of a very attractive return as the recovery gathered pace – even possibly the opportunity of a lifetime. As he scanned through a comprehensive list of outstanding corporate debt in issue it became clear that, even if one set fairly stringent criteria in terms of rating and maturity (no longer than four years), it ought to be possible to construct a well-spread portfolio with a yield of over 20%, especially in emerging markets where the credit risk on corporations was often significantly less than on the relevant sovereign credit.

Encouraged by Peter, the trustees, particularly Jenny Bingham, who also knew Mark Coombs personally, moved very quickly so that by the end of April a segregated account was set up and fully invested.

The result was a twelve-month gain of nearly 40%. In July of 2010 the segregated account was switched into Ashmore's Emerging Markets Corporate Fund, where it has continued to produce exceptional results.

Both Ashmore and Peter believe that there is still considerable mileage in this specialized investment field, with pockets of extraordinary opportunity remaining, especially in countries that are rich in natural resources, as commodity prices rise in response to the recovery in demand.

But what instructive conclusions might the average retail investor draw from the way that Peter is handling the investment of his personal fortune? It may come as a surprise that it has been many years, in fact the late 1970s, since Peter has made any attempt to "cherry pick" individual stocks for his personal portfolio. As he remarked himself:

> I used to try to pick the best stocks in the fund portfolios, but I always picked the wrong ones. Now I take my own money and invest it with that odd guy Peter Cundill. I can be more detached when I treat myself as an ordinary client.

Peter, justifiably, has great confidence in his own abilities, which only very occasionally wobbled, and so investing for himself in his own funds was simply obvious. What is perhaps more important is that the time that he did not waste in personal stock or bond selection was mainly devoted to "cherry picking" other managers who practised his own value discipline and then backing them with his own money. This is something that it is open to anyone. It is unlikely that there is a single serious mutual fund or money manager who does not publish detailed results, including his portfolio and a statement of his investment methodology, on a quarterly basis. Peter himself pores over these with great attention – both the ones in which he already has an interest and those he might consider. It seems probable that it is easier to identify winning fund managers than it is to pick winning stocks.

The great managers today are public figures, even household names. The emerging ones are revealed only by how they set about what they do and by their numbers. However, there is one additional feature about the way that Peter generally approaches the point of actually committing money to a manager – he prefers to invest when a good manager has suffered a bad patch. Old habits die hard and in terms of the individual manager selection he regards this element of timing as being analogous to a margin of safety.

Constrained though he is by the limitations imposed by the encroachments of Fragile X, Peter still lives a rich and fulfilling life. He never mopes. He goes to theatre and the ballet in his wheelchair and to most major exhibitions. He is an ardent rugby fan and materially supports the McGill University Rugby Club. There is an endless stream of visits and correspondence with those seeking financial help for endeavours of every kind and his generosity is extraordinary, with only a very slight bias in favour of athletics and investment. This year he has travelled to Bermuda for his family office meetings and made a four-day helicopter trip to Cornwall and the Scilly isles, visiting castles and gardens and following the Daphne du Maurier trail. He attended a dinner in his honour in Toronto, spending a happy week there seeing many old friends and colleagues and rejoicing in being a Canadian in Canada again, and visited Sicily for the first time to explore its architecture, antiquities, and culture. Long may all this continue!

The portrait of Peter by Peter Hendrick that hangs in the Mackenzie reception area.

Glossary of Terms with Peter Cundill's Comments

A

ACCOUNTING

"Accounting is nothing more than a language. There are two parts to this process: making statements and interpreting them. I've spend most of my career interpreting them. I know how you can tell fibs in a balance sheet. I can tell by the accounting whether a company is conservative or aggressive. It's a feeling."

ALWAYS CHANGE A WINNING GAME

The investment business is organic, based on a mix of financials, politics, human greed, and a huge dose of sentiment – not forgetting the urge to outdo the competition.

"Sir John Templeton said something to me and it stuck in my mind and I didn't do anything about it at the time. We were on a roll of fifteen years of wonderful results, no down years, a high compound rate of return and some money coming in. He said something which I think is correct, and that Graham also talks about; 'always change a winning game.' I didn't do it because I was on a roll then and I wasn't flexible enough. There is no investment rule that remains immutable except the margin of safety. There are always breaks and the trick is to begin to anticipate, if you can, where the break points will be and shift. Not the disciplines and not the framework but the tactics that are involved."

ANALYSIS

"There's almost too much information now. It boggles most shareholders and a lot of analysts. All I really need is a company's published reports and records; that plus a sharp pencil, a pocket calculator, and patience."

"Doing the analysis yourself gives you confidence buying securities when a lot of the external factors are negative. It gives you something to hang your hat on."

ANALYSTS

"I'd prefer not to know what the analysts think or to hear any inside information. It clouds one's judgement – I'd rather be dispassionate."

ANTITHESIS OF VALUE

"If you are under the impression that value investing does not include the use of derivatives, well you are wrong. Futures and option markets allow you to go short with less risk than used to be the case, so from time to time we use them as an offensive weapon to exploit what I call 'the antithesis of value,' where, for example, by any measure of value – not just our own value framework – a market is grotesquely out of alignment with reality. I first used the technique in the late 1980s buying puts on the Nikkei. It required nerve and patience, lots of both, but we made a lot of money in the long run. It is true that many value investors find a lot of difficulty doing the antithesis of value. But we've been doing it long enough that we are comfortable with it. We go short on markets, not individual securities."

B

BANKRUPTCIES

Chapter 7 of the Bankruptcy Reform Act deals with liquidation, while Chapter XI deals with a form of bankruptcy that involves a reorganization of a corporation's business affairs and assets. It is generally filed by companies that require time to restructure their debts. Chapter XI gives the debtor protection from creditors to allow the formulation of a plan of reorganization to be agreed on with the creditors. Similar schemes exist in most developed countries. Peter Cundill has used his commercial and accounting skills in looking at both forms of bankruptcy to evaluate either what may be salvaged in a liquidation or what value may be placed on a company's debt or equity as it emerges from Chapter XI.

"As regards the bankruptcy stuff, Marty Whitman is the senior proponent and he tends to start off in the senior debt, which is the safest part of the estate to be in, rather than the junior debt, or the equity."

BOOK VALUE

Otherwise known as carrying value, book value is the value of an asset as shown in the balance sheet and is based on original cost less depreciation. Historically a corporation's book value was defined as its total assets less intangible assets (such as goodwill) and liabilities. More recently book value has sometimes been calculated with goodwill and other intangibles included, which is anathema to a value investor. Dividing the book value by the number of shares outstanding gives book value per share and in the value investor framework this is an important figure to compare against the actual price per share (see Magic Sixes).

BRADY BONDS

Bonds are issued at a discount by the governments of developing countries, predominantly to replace defaulted syndicated bank debt, which is illiquid and represents a stumbling block to raising additional loans in international markets. Brady bonds are some of the most liquid of emerging market securities. They are named after former US Treasury Secretary Nicholas Brady, who sponsored the effort to restructure emerging market debt instruments. Most issuers have been Latin American countries.

BROKERS

"I go cold when someone tips me on a company. I like to start with a clean sheet: no one's word. No givens. I'm more comfortable when there are no brokers looking over my shoulder."

"They really can't afford to be contrarians. A major investment house can't afford to do research for five customers who won't generate a lot of commissions."

BUYOUTS

The purchase of a controlling interest in one corporation by another corporation or a private equity firm, in order to take over assets and/or operations. One of Peter's particular interests has been to study some of the problem buyouts over the past three decades, especially where significant leverage is involved.

"Some of these buyouts are going to go wrong, especially if we hit a recession, and then I'm going to have a lot to do."

C

CASH

Peter Cundill has always tended to hold large cash positions in his portfolios; at times as much as 40%.

"When there aren't a lot of net-net situations around, I get worried about the market and start to sell into cash. The tough market will force a lot of companies into a net-net situation and then I can put my money to good use."

CAPITAL MARKETS

Any market where debt or equity securities are traded.

"When the U.S. capital markets turn their attention to a foreign marketplace, they are like General Sherman marching through Georgia: they leave a few blades of black grass, so you'd better get there first."

CIGAR-BUTT INVESTING

The "cigar-butt" approach to investing comes from Warren Buffett: "If you buy a stock at a sufficiently low price, there will usually be some tick up in the fortunes of the business that gives you a chance to unload at a decent profit, even though the long-term performance of the business may be terrible. I call this the "cigar-butt" approach to investing. A cigar-butt found in the street, which has only one puff left in it, may not offer much of a smoke, but the bargain purchase will make that puff all profit."

CONSISTENCY

"If you base a fund's growth or a client's future on one or two potential skyrockets, you have to be prepared to live with the misfires. And I simply can't do that. I strive for consistency."

CREDIT

"If you can borrow money, then over time markets will be all right. It's only in periods like 1974 and 2009 when you cannot borrow at any rate of interest that markets are truly hazardous to your health because, without firm, co-ordinated, centralized action, the system is in danger of outright collapse."

CUNDILL'S COROLLARY

"There are cases when Cundill's corollary applies. That's when you're beyond Murphy's Law, which says that if anything can go wrong it will, and beyond O'Brien's Law, which says Murphy is an optimist. Cundill's corollary says that when Murphy's Law is still in play one should wait, but when things get so bad that you're really scared, that's the time to buy."

D

DEAD COMPANIES

"The companies I buy, when I buy them, are worth more to me dead than alive. I don't invest to see them die but I go in knowing that if I keep buying at my price and end up owning the companies, they will be worth more at liquidation than I paid for them."

DISCOUNTED CASH FLOWS

Discounted cash flow (DCF) analysis uses future free cash flow projections and discounts them (most often using the weighted average cost of capital) to arrive at a present value, which is used to evaluate the potential for investment. If the value arrived at through DCF analysis is higher than the current cost of the investment, the consensus is usually that the investment opportunity is a good one.

"When it comes to using discounted cash flows I have a firm view. I was reading some work and it uses discounted cash flows and some sophisticated stuff and I am not good enough at math to be able to work out that kind of stuff and I have sort of come back in my simple way to Graham who said if you can't add it, subtract it, multiply or divide it, then the math is too heavy. And the problem with this kind of cash flow is that it is simply a projection and, whatever the rate you choose to use, that will almost certainly shift on you. So you are trying to make two imprecise variables into a precise tool and that could get you into a whole mess of trouble"

E

EXTRA ASSETS

This has been a favourite focus of Peter Cundill's, particularly from the 1980s onwards when the pool of conventional net-nets and magic sixes had all but disappeared. Extra assets, or additional assets, are often to be found in companies such as insurance companies that own stock portfolios (traditionally valued at cost, not market) or real estate portfolios held at very low prices on the balance sheet.

"This started for me when Mutual Shares chieftain Mike Price, who used to be a pure net-net investor, began talking about something called the 'extra asset syndrome' or at least that is what I call it. It's taking, you might say, net-net one step farther, to look at all of a company's assets, figure the true value."

F

FIRST JOB/FIRST INVESTMENT

"I worked as an office boy for Wood Gundy in the summer of 1959 while at McGill. My first purchase was in a speculative mining stock and, within 48 hours, I had lost my complete investment of $500."

FIRST MUTUAL FUND

"On my twenty-first birthday my godfather gave me $1000 worth of Canadian Investment Fund, the oldest open-ended mutual fund in Canada. I didn't even know what a mutual fund was at the time, but when I cashed it in a few years later, it allowed me to have a wonderful year in Europe."

FORECASTING

"We don't do a lot of forecasting per se about where markets are going. I have been burned often enough trying. I only know of one investor, George Soros, who has been able to maintain very good records in anticipating markets and doing a whole lot of things simultaneously. It's as if he were not only a champion at tennis, but a champion squash player, a champion jai alai player, and generally a champion game player, where most of us in this business are good at doing only one part."

G

GLOBAL INVESTING

"To a Canadian, almost all stocks in the world are by definition foreign. And given the dearth of bargains today, it pays to search for them everywhere."

I

INDEPENDENCE

Peter Cundill has never been afraid to make his own decisions and by setting up his own fund management company he has been relatively free from external control and constraint. He doesn't follow investment trends or listen to the popular press about what is happening on "the street." He has travelled a lonely but profitable road. "He has strength as an independent; he doesn't want to be an operator." –Tim Price, chair of Hees

"Being willing to be the only one in the parade that's out of step. It's awfully hard to do, but Peter is disciplined. You have to be willing to wear bellbottoms when everyone else is wearing stovepipes." –Ross Southam, manager, McLeod Young Weir Ltd, Vancouver.

INSIDER INFORMATION

"When somebody is trying to give you information that you think might be a problem – what you want to do is shut your ears because it sounds like inside information and firstly it might get you into trouble and almost invariably it is wrong, so ignore it as best you can. If necessary say, 'don't talk to me anymore.'"

INVESTMENT FORMULA

"Mostly Graham, a little Buffett, and a bit of Cundill."

"I like to think that if I stick to my formula, my shareholders and I can make a lot of money without much risk."

"When I stray out of my comfort zone I usually get my head handed to me on a platter."

"I suspect that my thinking is an eclectic mix, not pure net-net because I couldn't do it anyway so you have to have a new something to hang your hat on. But the framework stays the same."

INVESTMENT STRATEGY

"I used to try and pick the best stocks in the fund portfolios, but I always picked the wrong ones. Now I take my own money and invest it with that odd guy Peter Cundill. I can be more detached when I treat myself as a normal client."

"If it is cheap enough, we don't care what it is."

"Why will someone sell you a dollar for 50 cents? Because in the short run, people are irrational on both the optimistic and pessimistic side."

INVESTORS

What type of investor is interested in Cundill Value Fund?

"I suppose on one hand it's the kind of investor who is interested in this style of investment – who understands and appreciates what value investment means. There is also the other kind of investor, who doesn't spend a lot of time worrying about what value investment means but just understands that this way, over time, you can develop useful returns with limited volatility."

What words of advice would Peter give to investors interested in international investing right now?

"Try to pick a fund manager who has a well-defined strategy, has been through these things before, and go invest and stay with him."

L

LIBOR

London interbank offered rate. The rate at which banks borrow unsecured funds from each other in the London wholesale market – usually overnight. The average interest rate paid for such funds is computed daily for all the principal international currencies and provides a clear indication of the real cost of short term credit.

M

THE MAGIC SIXES

"The magic sixes" are something Peter learned about from Norman Weiner of Oppenheimer in the 1970s. They are companies trading at less than 0.6 times book value (less than 60% of book value), 6 times earnings or less, and with dividend yields of 6% or more. At that time there were hundreds of publicly traded companies in the U.S. that met the test. It is a quick formula that allows one to screen any stock market in the world to see if it may have any value opportunities, applying the Graham fundamentals.

MANTRAS

"All we try to do is buy a dollar for 40 cents."

"In our style of doing things, patience is patience is patience."

"One of the dangers about net-net investing is that if you buy a net-net that begins to lose money your net-net goes down and your capacity to be able to make a profit becomes less secure. So the trick is not necessarily to predict what the earnings are going to be but to have a clear conviction that the company isn't going bust and that your margin of safety will remain intact over time."

MARGIN OF SAFETY

A principle of investing in which the investor only purchases securities when the market price is significantly below his estimate of the intrinsic value; the difference between the two is the margin of safety. Its careful practice does not guarantee a profitable investment but it significantly reduces the downside risk. The term was popularized by Benjamin Graham (known as "the father of value investing") and his followers, most notably Warren Buffett.

"The difference between the price we pay for a stock and its liquidation value gives us a margin of safety. This kind of investing is one of the most effective ways of achieving good long term results."

MARKETS

"The market is a weighing machine, and if you buy cheaply enough, sooner or later the true value of an investment will be realised."

"If there's a bad stock market, I'll inevitably go back in too early. Good times last longer than we think but so do bad times."

"When the market falls sharply, it doesn't distinguish between the good girls and the bad girls."

"You need to have bad markets to set the stage for the 40% annual increases. If we had good markets forever, I'd be dead."

"Markets can be overvalued and keep getting expensive, or undervalued and keep getting cheap. That's why investing is an art form, not a science."

"I'm agnostic on where the markets will go. I don't have a view. Our task is to find undervalued global securities that are trading well below their intrinsic value. In other words, we follow the strict Benjamin Graham approach to investing."

MOAT INVESTING

The term "economic moat" was coined by Warren Buffett. It refers to the ability of a business to maintain a competitive advantage over its competitors in order to protect long term profits and market share. A good example of a competitive advantage would be a low-cost advantage such as cheap access to raw materials, cheap transport to market, or a very strong brand.

"I would say that the problem with big businesses that have moats around them is they tend to over-expand."

N

NET ASSET VALUE (NAV)

The value of a corporation's assets minus its liabilities. For analytical purposes this figure is often divided by the number of shares outstanding to give the net asset value per share so that it can be readily compared with the actual stock price per share.

NET-NET

A value investing technique in which a company is valued solely on its net current assets. The net-net investing method focuses on current assets, taking cash and cash equivalents at full value, reducing accounts receivable for doubtful accounts, and reducing inventories to liquidation values. Total liabilities are then deducted from the adjusted current assets to get the company's net-net value. This method was introduced by Benjamin Graham.

NEVER SHOOT INTO THE BROWN

"My father was a very good shot, and he always said 'never shoot into the brown.' In other words, never shoot into a flock of birds without first choosing a single bird – at least in your mind."

NEW LOWS

"Search out the new lows, not the new highs. Read the *Outstanding Investors Digest* to find out what Mason Hawkins is doing or Mike Price is doing. You know good poets borrow and great poets steal. So see what you can find. General reading – keep looking at the news to see what's troubled. Experience and curiosity is a really winning combination."

"What differentiates us from other money managers with a similar style is that we're comfortable with new lows.

NIGHTMARES AND IPOS

"IPOs [Initial Public Offerings] for the most part are dreams engendered by the hope that the pro forma estimates will be met. We deal to a certain extent in nightmares that everyone knows about."

NOBODY LISTENING

"Many people consider value investing dull and as boring as watching paint dry. As a consequence value investors are not always listened to, especially in a stock market bubble. Investors are often in too much of a hurry to latch on to growth stocks to stop and listen because they're afraid of being left out. Very often it would be a good thing if they were."

NOVEMBER RAIN

"I began to get into the practice when I was living in Vancouver in November, the time when it begins to rain – I would travel to the place with the worst stock market in the world in the first eleven months of the year. Sometimes the weather was even worse but it was very valuable."

O

OSMOSIS

"I don't just calculate value using net-net. Actually there are many different ways but you have to use what I call osmosis – you have got to feel your way. That is the art form, because you are never going to be right completely; there is no formula that will ever get you there on its own. Osmosis is about intuition and about discipline and about all the other things that are not quantifiable. So can you learn it? Yes, you can learn it, but it's not a science, it's an art form. The portfolio is a canvas to be painted and filled in."

P

PATIENCE

"When times aren't good I'm still there. You find bargains among the unpopular things, the things that everybody hates. The key is that you must have patience."

R

RETURNS

Over the past thirty-five years, since its inception in 1974, the Mackenzie Cundill Value Fund (Series A) has delivered an average annual compound rate of return of 13.2%, while the MSCI World Index returns in Canadian dollar terms for the same period are 10.8%. Another way of looking at it, a $10,000 investment in the Mackenzie Cundill Value Fund (Series A) at inception with distributions re-invested would have grown to $927,522, net of fees, compared to the MSCI World Index of $437,438, before any costs, for the same period (see Appendix Four).

RISK

"We try not to lose. But we don't want to try too hard. The losses, of course, work against you in establishing decent compound rates of return. And I hope we won't have them. But I don't want to be so risk-averse that we are always trying too hard not to lose."

"I've lived, I suppose globally and I've travelled pretty extensively. So I don't really see much more risk investing in foreign countries than I do in investing in North America."

RUNNING

"What's most useful is that I can do my running and start thinking about what I've been reading. So I can do two things at once – beside chew gum and walk. It's a nice way of getting the exercise."

"About fifty percent of my time is spent reading, and running is useful for digesting it all. I run almost every day, but I hope not to the point of obsession. I've been known to have the odd dry martini now and then as well."

S

SELLING

"I am confident in buying because I am dealing in reality. The real problem is trying to figure out when to sell."

"I am a bear market buyer; I like to sell into market strength."

"When a stock doubles, sell half – then what you have is a free position. Then it becomes more of an art form. When you sell depends on individual circumstances."

STEADY RETURNS

"All I know is that if you can end up with a 20% track record over a longer period of time, the compound rates of return are such that the amounts are staggering. But a lot of investors want excitement, not steady returns. Most people don't see making money as grinding it out, doing it as efficiently as possible. If we have a strong market over the next six months and the fund begins to drop behind and there isn't enough to do, people will say Cundill's lost his touch, he's boring."

SUM OF THE PARTS

Valuing a company by determining what its divisions would be worth if it was broken up and spun off or acquired by another company.

T

TEN BAGGER

"Ten bagger" is an investment term coined by Peter Lynch in his book *One Up on Wall Street*. It refers to any investment that becomes worth ten times its original purchase price.

TIMING: "THERE'S ALWAYS SOMETHING TO DO"

"You know, it all depends on your entry point and the situation on the day – which is what Graham was really doing – and being flexible. If I had started doing net-net investing in 1973 then I never would have lasted to 1975 in the business. Stocks would have just gotten cheaper and I would have died on the vine and would have had to go back and be a chartered accountant, which would have been a laugh both professionally and for me. Yet Irving Kahn gave me some advice many years ago when I was bemoaning the fact that according to my criteria there was nothing to do. He said, 'there is always something to do. You just need to look harder, be creative and a little flexible.'"

V

VALUE INVESTING

"I don't think I want us to become too fashionable. In some ways value investing is boring and most investors don't want a boring life – they want some action: win, lose, or draw."

"I think the best decisions are made on the basis of what your tummy tells you. The Jesuits argue reason before passion. I argue reason and passion. Intellect and intuition. It's a balance."

"I try to buy securities below their seeming liquidation value. The idea is that if I get something that is worth a dollar for fifty cents I'll do alright."

"I pay much more attention to the balance sheet than the profit and loss statement and am always looking for hidden assets on the books."

"We do liquidation analysis and liquidation analysis only."

"Ninety to 95% of all my investing meets the Graham tests. The times I strayed from a rigorous application of this philosophy I got myself into trouble."

"But what do you do when none of these companies is available? The trick is to wait through the crisis stage and into the boredom stage. Things will have settled down by then and values will be very cheap again."

"I suppose I'm a bit dogmatic about that, but I believe you can get high, consistent returns by following this methodology."

"Who says you can't join value and growth at the hip?"

"We customarily do three tests: one of them asset-based – the NAV, using the company's balance sheet. The second is the sum of the parts, which I think is probably the most important part that goes into the balance sheet I'm creating. And then a future NAV, which is making a stab (which I am always suspicious about) at what you think the business might be doing in three years from now."

W

WORKING LIFE

"I've been doing this for thirteen years. And I love it. I'm lucky to have the kind of life where the differentiation between work and play is absolutely zilch. I have no idea whether I'm working or whether I'm playing."

"I knew I wasn't spending enough time in my head office about eighteen months ago when I arrived back in the main office that bears my name and the receptionist looked at me and said, 'what can I do for you, sir?'"

"My wife says I'm a workaholic, but my colleagues say I haven't worked for twenty years. My work is my play."

Z

ZEROES (AND HEROES)

"I bought stuff at 3.5 cents once and I thought it can't go down to zero. It can."

"I think that the worst one that we have had was Cable & Wireless. It had sold a number of its telephone companies in Hong Kong and Australia and in their UK base and had lots of cash and a stand alone operation in the Caribbean. But they had ambitions in the fibre optic business, which was blowing cash. So we said, look they've got cash, we have got a valuable business, and let's assume the fibre optic business is worth zero – it wasn't, it was worth much less than zero, so we had our heads handed to us. We were able to recover a little bit but it was a bad investment. And that is why you diversify, even when you believe in the merits of concentration."

"John Templeton said something to me a couple of years ago – he said if you are right 60% of the time and wrong 40% you will be a hero and if you are right 40% and wrong 60% you will be a bum. But I am sure he used more gracious language than that."

Appendix 1
Some major figures in Peter Cundill's investment world

WARREN BUFFETT

Warren Buffett, born in 1930, is an American investor and one of the most successful in the world, ranked as the world's third richest individual in 2010. Often referred to as "The Sage of Omaha," where he lives, he runs Berkshire Hathaway. He is well known for his adherence to Graham's value principles and was a student of Graham's at Columbia.

When asked if he would look beyond the US border in his search for a new chief investment officer, Mr Buffett said he wouldn't rule out a Canadian candidate: "Someone like a Peter Cundill."

BENJAMIN GRAHAM, 1894–1976

An American economist and professional investor, Graham is considered to be the originator of the concept of value investing. He started lecturing at the Columbia Business School in 1928 and later, in collaboration with David Dodd, wrote *Security Analysis*, considered the theoretical bible for value investment. Graham's disciples have included Jean-Marie Eveillard, Warren Buffett, Charles Brandes, Irving Kahn, Walter Schloss, Michael Price, and, of course, Peter

Cundill. Graham had such an overwhelming influence on his students that two of them, Buffett and Kahn, named their sons after him.

"Graham believed that the value of a company had almost no relationship to its stock price. The application of his theories demanded detailed analysis and a lot of patience and discipline."

"I wonder, if Benjamin Graham were writing today, if he would have some chapters on the antithesis of value."

"At the beginning I always thought of Graham as the guy that did net-nets and was inflexible. He was actually a remarkably flexible thinker. If you go through the five editions or whatever of *Security Analysis*, there were times when he talked about net-nets and there were times when he didn't talk about them. If Graham were writing today for a sixth edition what, I wonder, would he talk about? I think he would have to spend time on internationalisation. The world has not bypassed America, because that is where it all started. It is still the heartland of capitalism, but there are now any number of international securities to invest in and the disclosures are much better. The second thing he would do is to talk about derivatives and about accounting issues. So I think that the thrust of what he would now say is be flexible within the framework, be international and, above all, which has been my mantra from the very beginning, be patient."

IRVING KAHN

With nearly eighty years of experience, Kahn is possibly the oldest financial analyst on Wall Street. A value investor, he is still chair of Kahn Brothers Group, Inc., the privately owned investment advisory and broker-dealer firm that he founded in 1978 with his sons, Alan and Thomas, and still carries out an active role at the company at the age of 105. Kahn has the distinction of being both a student of Graham's and for a period his research assistant. Irving Kahn has been a close confidant and mentor to Peter.

MICHAEL F. PRICE

A renowned money manager, Price learned about finance as a $200-a-week research assistant under Max Heine, the founder of Mutual Shares. Heine was an early advocate of Graham's value investment methods and Price followed suit, earning a reputation for buying undervalued and distressed companies. He took over control of Mutual Shares following Heine's death and sold it in 1996 to Franklin Resources for $670 million. Price now manages the private firm of MFP Investors, with $1.6 billion under management, much of it his own money. Peter served on the Mutual Shares board for a number of years.

GEORGE SOROS

Not a value investor as such, but an investor for whom Peter has immense admiration and respect. His Quantum Fund has been spectacularly successful. The two have met to exchange thoughts on a number of occasions over the years.

"I only know of one investor, George Soros, who has been able to maintain very good records in anticipating markets and doing a whole lot of things simultaneously. It's as if he were not only a champion at tennis, but a champion squash player, a champion jai alai player and generally a champion game player, where most of us in this business are good at doing only one part."

JOHN TEMPLETON, 1912–2008

Templeton was an American investor and a mutual fund pioneer. Graduating from Yale in 1934, he won a Rhodes Scholarship to Oxford and added an MA in Law. Templeton became a billionaire by pioneering the use of globally diversified mutual funds. His Templeton Growth Fund, established in 1954, was among the first to invest in Japan in the middle of the 1960s. He was knighted in 1987.

Sir John Templeton was one of Peter's first investors in the Cundill Value Fund; he was also a great mentor.

PREM WATSA

Born in 1950 in Hyderabad, India, he is the founder, chair, and chief executive of Fairfax Financial Holdings, based in Toronto, and has been called the "Canadian Warren Buffett." He is a CFA charter holder, a graduate of the Indian Institute of Technology with a degree in chemical engineering, and the holder of an MBA from the Richard Ivey School of Business of the University of Western Ontario. He is a member of the Advisory Board for the Richard Ivey School of Business.

MARTIN J. WHITMAN

An American investment advisor and a strong critic of the direction of recent changes in generally accepted accounting principles (GAAP) in the US. He is founder, co-chief investment officer, and portfolio manager of the Third Avenue Value Fund. Whitman is a 1949 graduate of Syracuse University, which recently renamed its School of Management after him. He is an adjunct faculty member at Yale School of Management. He is regarded by Peter as one of the foremost experts on distressed debt and on innovation within a value investment framework.

Appendix 2
Investments held by Peter Cundill entities as of 31 July 2010

ABC North America Deep-Value Fund
Ashmore Emerging Markets Corporate High Yield Fund
Church House Deep-Value Fund
Cundill Distressed Fund Ltd – Class A
Cundill Global Value Limited Partnership Class A
Cundill International Company Ltd – Class A
Deltec Recovery Fund Limited Partnership
IGM Financial Inc.
Kennox Asset Management
KJH Strategic Investors Fund
Longleaf Partners Funds
Mackenzie Cundill Canadian Securities Fund – Series A
Mackenzie Cundill Canadian Securities Fund – Series O
Mackenzie Cundill Recovery Fund – Series O
Mackenzie Cundill Value Fund – Series A
Mackenzie Cundill Value Fund – Series O
Mackenzie Universal Canadian Value Fund
McElvaine Investment Trust Series B
Morant Wright Japan Fund A Shares
New Silk Road Fund

Nielsen Global Value Fund (Luxemburg)
Orbis Leveraged Equity Fund
Overstone Global Equity Fund C
Pacific and General Investments Inc.
Penta Asia Fund
Phoenix Asset Management Partners Ltd
Preservation Capital Trust
Steel Partners Japan Strategic Offshore Fund
Steel Partners Offshore Fund Ltd
Thai Focused Equity Fund Ltd
Unison Capital Partners II Limited Partnership
Van Biema Value Fund Limited Partnership
Ward Ferry Asia Fund Ltd
West Creek Partners Fund

Appendix 3
Net-net work sheet designed by Peter in 1975 and still in use today

Peter Cundill & Associates Ltd.
INVESTMENT APPRAISAL FORM -- NET NET
24-Apr-96

Analyst: FPC/TM/AWM Contact: Dr JC Matherly Symbol: OTC listed

Company: **Neue Zuricher Zeitung** Currency: Sfr

Current Price: 54,500 Total Mkt Value: 218.0 Year End: Dec 95

		Dec95	Dec94
Business: Premier German newspaper in Switzerland	Registered shares	4,000	4,000

Sedol #:

Major Shareholders:
Swiss Residents - 80%

EPS	Dec95	Dec94	Dec93	Dec92	Dec91
1					
2					
3					
4	4,880	6,105	2,760	651	1,204

PROFIT & LOSS ANALYSIS
(In: MILLIONS)

	Dec95	Dec94	Dec93	Dec92	Dec91
Revenues	355.3	336.7	319.1	170.5	179.3
Inc before x-ord	19.5	24.4	11.0	2.6	4.8
Net Income	19.5	24.4	11.0	2.6	4.8
EPS (before x-ord)	4,880	6,105	2,760	651	1,204
EPS (incl x-ord)	4,880	6,105	2,760	651	1,204
Dividend P.S.	330	330	300	na	na
Price Range:					
High	50,000	39,500	33,000	NA	NA
Low	40,250	32,500	29,750	NA	NA
Volume		NA	NA	NA	NA

BALANCE SHEET
(In: MILLIONS)

	Dec95	Dec94	Dec93	Dec92	Dec91
Cash and securities	27.2	40.7	30.9	30.9	47.6
Other current assets	66.3	55.4	50.0	28.3	31.2
Current Liabil.	(62.2)	(50.7)	(49.4)	(51.0)	(54.3)
Working Capital	31.4	45.4	31 4	8.2	24.5
Less: LT Debt	(45.5)	(71.2)	(89.8)	(21.9)	(21.9)
Pension liab	0.0	0.0	0.0	0.0	0.0
Other	0.0	0.0	0.0	0.0	0.0
Add: Equity invest. (cost)	118.2	107.9	102.3	0.0	0.0
Other investments	0.0	0.0	0.0	113.0	86.5
Net Net Working Capital	104.0	82.1	43.9	99.3	89.1
Net Net Working Capital P.S.	26,011	20,525	10,983	24,827	22,268

Add: Net Fixed Assets	276.7	290.6	300.4	89.1	98.2
Int. Ass (incl def chgs)	0.5	1.0	1 4	0.0	0.0
Other Assets	0.0	0.0	0.0	0.0	0.0
Less: Def. Inc. Tax	0.0	0.0	0.0	0.0	0.0
Min. Int.	(20.1)	(19.7)	(18.2)	0.0	0.0
Untaxed reserves	0.0	0.0	0.0	0.0	0.0
Allow. and provisions	(58.8)	(60.5)	(56.3)	(88.3)	(93.8)
Shrhldrs Equity	302.3	293.5	271 4	100.1	93.5
Shareholders Equity P.S.	75,580	73,375	67,840	25,031	23,383

CASH FLOW ANALYSIS

(In: MILLIONS)					
Net Profit	19.5	24.4	11.0	2.6	4.8
Deprec & Amort	25.8	24.9	24.8	13.6	12.5
Other non-cash	0.0	0.0	0.0	0.0	0.0
Gross Cash Flow	45.3	49.3	35.8	16.2	17.3
Gross Cash Flow P.S.	11,330	12,320	8,960	4,061	4,329
CAPEX	12.4	18.4			

Neue Zuricher Zeitung

OTHER DATA

Employees	1,602
Shareholders	1,356
Debt/Equity Ratio	15.1%
Return on Sales	5.5%
Return on S.E.	6.5%
Return on Price Paid	22.7%
Price/Earnings	11.2
Price/cashflow	4.8
Current Yield	0.6%

	Dec95	Dec94	Dec93	Dec92	Dec91
INSURANCE VALUE PER DR MATHERLY					
Market				147.0	
Cost				0.0	
Diff				147.0	
Per Sh.				36,750.00	
Stated insurance values	462.0	430.0	406.0		
PENSION FUND					
Assets	NA	NA	NA	NA	NA
Accum Bene Oblig					
Proj Bene Oblig					
Amount on B/S					
Invest ROR					
LIFO					
Amount	NA	NA	NA	NA	NA
Per Share	NA	NA	NA	NA	NA
NOL					
Amount	NA	NA	NA	NA	NA
Per Share	NA	NA	NA	NA	NA

Other Comments:

Days of invent.	15	12	12	NA	NA
Days of rec'ls	47	45	40	NA	NA

Voting/Registration:

Each shareholder is restricted to a maximum of 30 votes. 17.6% of shareholders are not registered. Registration requirements are somewhat draconian, residence in certain Swiss cantons and membership in any Swiss liberal party (this is somewhat relaxed from the past).

Dividends:

Dividends are only paid out to registered shareholders. We have not been able to collect. Unpaid dividends remain in retained earnings.

Appendix 4
Performance chart showing the Mackenzie Cundill Value Fund measured against the MSCI World benchmark (C$)

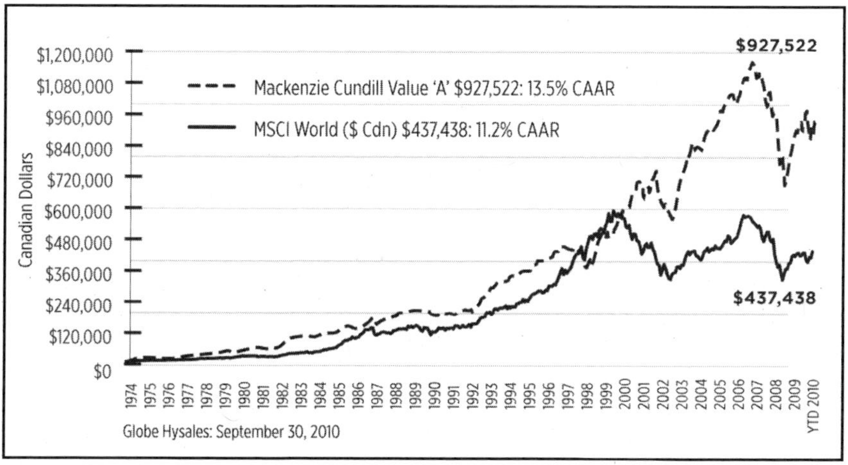

Appendix 5
Transcription of journal on p. 2

Racquets and Rumours

Sometimes you don't seem to focus on one thing long enough.

Aug 22/82 – Up at 10:30 to snuggle. Did yoga and other exercises. Nice walk with Joanie. Worked well. Bed by 7:30

Aug 23/82 – Up at 6:00 to run 3 ½ miles and exercise. Lunch with Tom Lockes re banking. Saw Danny Pekarsky. Good chat at 5 with Tony Novelly re Cities Service and Peter Ackerman. Markets way up – my stocks languish.

Sometimes nothing is more misleading than personal experience. A successful man is likely to be a forlorn and alien figure when his whole world begins to fail.

In a time of falling prices bankruptcies are an important factor for a great debt burden to be reduced.

In all bureaucracies there are three implacable spirits –

- self perpetuation
- expansion
- incessant demand for more power

Index